Shawn Arseneau

Junction Analysis

Shawn Arseneau

Junction Analysis

Representing Junctions through Asymmetric Tensor Diffusion

VDM Verlag Dr. Müller

Imprint

Bibliographic information by the German National Library: The German National Library lists this publication at the German National Bibliography; detailed bibliographic information is available on the Internet at http://dnb.d-nb.de.

Cover image: www.purestockx.com

Publisher:
VDM Verlag Dr. Müller Aktiengesellschaft & Co. KG, Dudweiler Landstr. 125 a, 66123 Saarbrücken, Germany,
Phone +49 681 9100-698, Fax +49 681 9100-988,
Email: info@vdm-verlag.de

Produced in USA and UK by:
Lightning Source Inc., La Vergne, Tennessee, USA
Lightning Source UK Ltd., Milton Keynes, UK
BookSurge LLC, 5341 Dorchester Road, Suite 16, North Charleston, SC 29418, USA

ISBN: 978-3-8364-9101-3

Acknowledgements

First, I would like to thank my supervisor Professor Jeremy Cooperstock for his invaluable direction and guidance in helping me complete the Ph.D. His continued help and support throughout my time at McGill have been greatly appreciated. Moreover, I would like to thank Professor Cooperstock for his meticulous and critical reading of all of my technical documents over the years, including this work, as well as for always challenging me to see new ways of bridging theory and application.

I would also like to thank Professors James Clark and Michael Langer for their advice and expertise in aiding me direct my thesis research towards its final form. In addition, I thank Professor Kaleem Siddiqi for his technical feedback and discussion on the topic of relaxation labeling.

I am also pleased to acknowledge the Centre for Intelligent Machines staff: Jan Binder, Cynthia Davidson and Marlene Gray, for their continued assistance over the years.

The early financial support through FQRNT, *Le Fonds Québécois de la Recherche sur la Nature et lest Technologies* is gratefully acknowledged.

For the help in correcting the French translation of this abstract, I'd like to thank both Marc Labrèche and Stéphane Pelletier.

Furthermore, I would like to thank Melita Hadzagic, Casey Lambert and Alessio Salerno for their friendship and mutual support in helping me realize this thesis.

My parents deserve my sincere appreciation for their unwavering confidence and support in my ability to pursue a doctorate degree.

Finally, to my wife Christie, to whom I dedicate this work, for her understanding, patience and encouragement, without whom I would not have been able to complete this work. Words alone cannot express my gratefulness for all that she has sacrificed over the years in my pursuit of a Ph.D.

Claim of Originality

The ideas expressed in this thesis, to the best of the author's knowledge, are original.[1] The contributions of this thesis are as follows:

- a method of transforming symmetric gradient information into an asymmetric representation

- an iterative update framework that enforces local support in an asymmetric manner

- a comparison of the effects of enforcing local support based on the estimates at the voting and receiving node

- a method of transforming a tensor-based directional distribution function into a 2D weight map

- a comparison of the effects of propagating a node's entire structural estimate versus a novel inward-based approach

- a mechanism to transform scalar, vector and tensor fields into appropriate input for the proposed method

- an error measure based on both direction and saliency designed specifically to compare competing local structural estimates

- an investigation of the conditions under which occlusion could potentially be identified in the 3D domain

---

[1]Some of the proposed methods and results in this document have been published previously [3,4].

List of Abbreviations

1D-DDF	One Dimensional, Directional Distribution Function (Scalar Form)
ATD	Asymmetric Tensor Diffusion
DDF	Directional Distribution Function
DTI	Diffusion Tensor Imaging
IB	Inward Ballot
ODF	Orientational Distribution Function
PO	Perceptual Organization
RAWM	Rotated Averaging Wedge Method
RC	Receiver-Centered
RC-DDF	Receiver-Centered, DDF Ballot
RC-IB	Receiver-Centered, Inward Ballot
RL	Relaxation Labeling
ST	Structure Tensor
TF	Tensor Field
TF-DDF	Tensor Field, Directional Distribution Function (Tensor Form)
TV	Tensor Voting
VC	Voter-Centered
VC-DDF	Voter-Centered, DDF Ballot
VC-IB	Voter-Centered, Inward Ballot

Contents

List of Figures

List of Tables

Chapter 1

Introduction

Junction is a general term given to points where multiple contours meet. Such points form important features in many computer vision applications. For example, interpolation algorithms make use of junctions to group sparse and noisy data in 3D scene reconstruction or to distinguish objects within a stereo depth map [57]. In image enhancement, connected contours between junctions denote boundaries over which smoothing should be inhibited [82]. Junctions also provide salient features for key points in fingerprint analysis, occlusion in motion segmentation, as well as defect detection in lumber inspection [36, 59, 74].

In the image domain, junctions are identified using the gradient information. The gradient represents a local contour estimate, therefore junctions are characterized by the presence of multiple gradient-based contours. In terms of structural elements, a junction can occur when contours split, merge or intersect. To depict all of these different configurations, the representation of local gradient information must be flexible enough to characterize multiple directional estimates. It must also be able to assign each estimate with a measure of certainty. For example, the intersection of a horizontal and vertical line forms a '+' shaped junction. The local representation should depict four estimates along the north, south, east and west directions as well as their relative certainty based on the original certainties of the lines. The directional distribution function (DDF) provides such a representation by collecting contour estimates into a directional histogram. The value at each of the angular bins represents the certainty of a gradient structure directed along the bin. Using this representation, the angular bins associated with local maxima provide directional estimates that are used in the classification step of junction

1

analysis.

Methods that transform the gradient information of an image into a DDF may be classified as either convolution or diffusion techniques. The former convolves rotated versions of a filter with the image data, similar to template matching. Many methods use the convolution results directly to populate the DDF, such as with Gabor filters. However, it is not uncommon to require further processing of this data prior to the initialization of the DDF. For example, the rotated averaging wegde method (RAWM) performs a first-order derivative calculation on the convolution results prior to populating the DDF. The features extracted from the resulting DDFs are then used either directly or in a multiscale framework for the junction classification step [45]. The convolution approach is useful in identifying patterns known *a priori*; however, several filter banks are often required to identify structures properly [31]. Also, errors in the directional estimates occur if the gradient-based contour does not coincide with the center of the window over which the convolution takes place.

In contrast, diffusion methods distribute local gradient information to its neighbors and then combine this data using specialized amalgamation techniques. In general, diffusion methods enforce *local support*, which is defined as strengthening common structural estimates while weakening all others. In terms of junction analysis, this implies contours are identified only if a majority of the neighboring points support this hypothesis. There are several different amalgamation techniques available depending on the requirements of the application. For example, tensor voting uses tensor addition, which is computationally inexpensive, while relaxation labeling allows for multiple orientation estimates at the expense of higher memory requirements [9,52]. Another advantage of diffusion techniques is that they are capable of populating structural estimates among both sparse and noisy data.

The problem is that both the convolution and diffusion methods are initialized with gradient information directly, which is *symmetric*. This means that local structures are represented using *two* vectors with each pointing in opposite directions, normal to the gradient edge. If the original data is symmetric, then the final results will also be symmetric. Consequently, the local structural representations will only be able to portray an *even* number of directional vectors. This implies that symmetric-based methods are unable to represent *asymmetric* junctions, which are defined as the merging of an *odd* number of contours such as a 'Y'

2

or 'T'-shaped junction. Without the capability to account for both symmetric and asymmetric junctions, incorrect estimates of the local structures are propagated into the final results. For example, contour end-points, which are asymmetric in that they are characterized by a single directional estimate, will diffuse outward after each iteration step with no stopping criteria. This means that every contour in the image will lengthen over time creating increasing numbers of false junction locations throughout the data space.

This dissertation proposes a two-step approach to represent asymmetric structure through an iterative process. The first step transforms the initial symmetric gradient information into an asymmetric, directional voting field, which is then distributed to its neighboring nodes in the form of ballots. The second step, described in Chapter 3, involves an iterative framework that diffuses these ballots based on local support as well as a custom weighting map and propagates information asymmetrically. Chapter 4 investigates several modules for the ability to create or maintain asymmetric structures. Chapter 5 describes experiments that compare the proposed method with convolution and diffusion techniques. Chapter 6 tests the proposed approach against real-world data as well as discusses the application domains for this work. Chapter 7 proposes directions for future research. Before delving into the details of the proposed approach, it is helpful to review some background of convolution and diffusion methods. This review is provided in Chapter 2.

Chapter 2

Literature Review

2.1 Convolution Methods

To identify asymmetric junctions, in particular those from image data, convolution methods must first be explored. For consistency of terminology, *direction* refers to the angle of a vector in $\Re^2$ with respect to the x-axis, ranging between $[0, 2\pi)$, while *orientation* is π-periodic ranging between $[0, \pi)$ as in the term 'horizontal orientation.' *Symmetry* refers to the geometric interpretation with respect to gradient-based contours, as in mirror-symmetric patterns rather than the concept of symmetric matrices.

To discern between the various types of junctions, local gradient patterns must first be inferred. This is described best through the terminology of *orientation analysis*, which, in its most general form is used to identify *oriented patterns* within a sub-region of data.[1] A useful tool to describe such information is the directional distribution function (DDF),[2] which provides a representation of the overall gradient-based directional topography. This representation depicts local maxima as estimates that align with the underlying gradient structure.

Several different forms can be used for the DDF. In diffusion-tensor imaging (DTI), a single tensor is used to represent the orientation of fiber tracks in the brain [7] while in many junction detection schemes the DDF is a discrete set of

---

[1] Oriented patterns in this work refer to sub-regions within the region of interest that exhibit a collection of gradient edges with a high degree of parallelism, similar to the concept of texture flow [9].

[2] The directional distribution function is an angular-based representation of local structure that reflects the certainty of a structure, namely lines and edges, along a given direction.

angular bins that are populated by results of a convolution step [75, 85]. The former method will be discussed in Section 2.2, while the convolution approach is now examined in further detail.

When using a convolution scheme, the DDF is initialized by the results of convolutions with rotated quadrature pairs of kernels, such as those depicted in Figure 2.1. The data is then recorded into angular bins similar to an orientation histogram [27]. This process is illustrated in Figure 2.2 using the wedge filter against a white corner swatch [75]. As the quadrature pair is rotated, the energy is recorded into the associated angular bin, as in Figures 2.2(f-i). In polar form, the radial component denotes the response or *saliency* of the kernel pair with respect to data at the given angle. As expected, this template matching approach should exhibit strong responses corresponding to local maxima when the underlying pattern best matches the design of the filters. As in this example, strong responses are exhibited when the filter is aligned with the two step-edges and is depicted as local maxima in the DDF. These maxima indicate the presence of dominant and recessive oriented patterns from the original input.[3]

2.1.1 Gabor Filters

The features exhibited in the DDF depend upon the choice of convolution kernel. The most common approach for calculating local gradient or orientation information is by convolving the image data with a specialized kernel, such as the Sobel mask or a quadrature pair of Gabor filters [31]. The goal is to balance the accuracy required for the orientation estimates against computational requirements of the application. For example, a simple 3x3 Sobel operator is computationally inexpensive. In contrast, Gabor filters employ a quadrature pair of kernels to address both even- and odd-phased gradients, are less susceptible to noise on account of the embedded Gaussian window, and can be adapted to varying scales [31]. Equation 2.1 defines the two-dimensional Gabor filter.

$$G\left(x,y\right) = \frac{1}{\sqrt{2\pi\sigma_x\sigma_y}} e^{-1/2\left(\frac{X^2}{\sigma_x} + \frac{Y^2}{\sigma_y}\right)} \cos\left(2\pi fX + P\right) \qquad (2.1)$$

---

[3]Patterns may refer to several different phenomena; however, in the field of junction analysis, it refers to gradient-based contours.

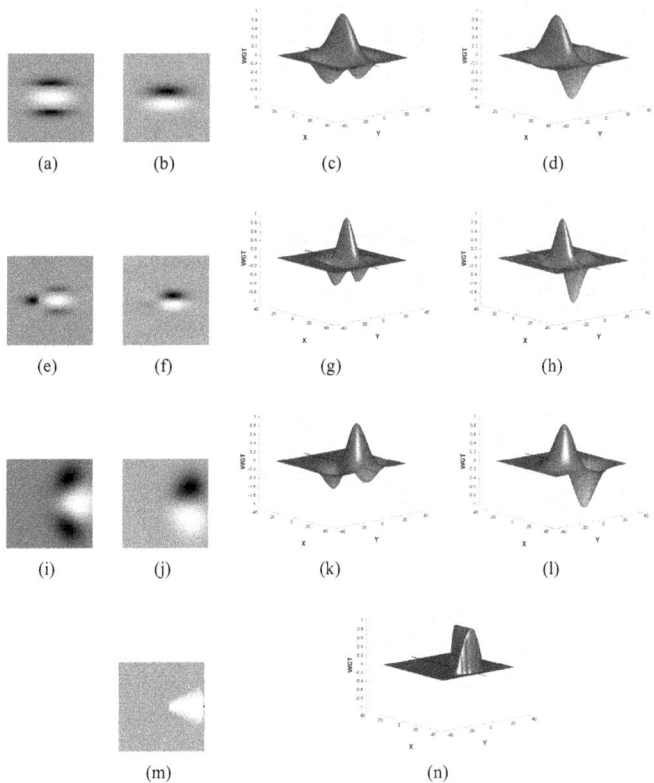

Figure 2.1: (1st and 3rd columns) are the even-phased kernels along $\theta=0^o$ and (2nd and 4th columns) are the corresponding odd-phased kernels. (a-d) is the Gabor, (e-h) one-sided [61], (i-l) wedge filters [75] and (m and n) the rotated averaging wedge method (RAWM) [85]. The first two columns are top-views of the last two columns respectively, where the first two columns denote the numeric values in grayscale (-1=black, 1=white) and the last two columns help visualize the lobe shapes.

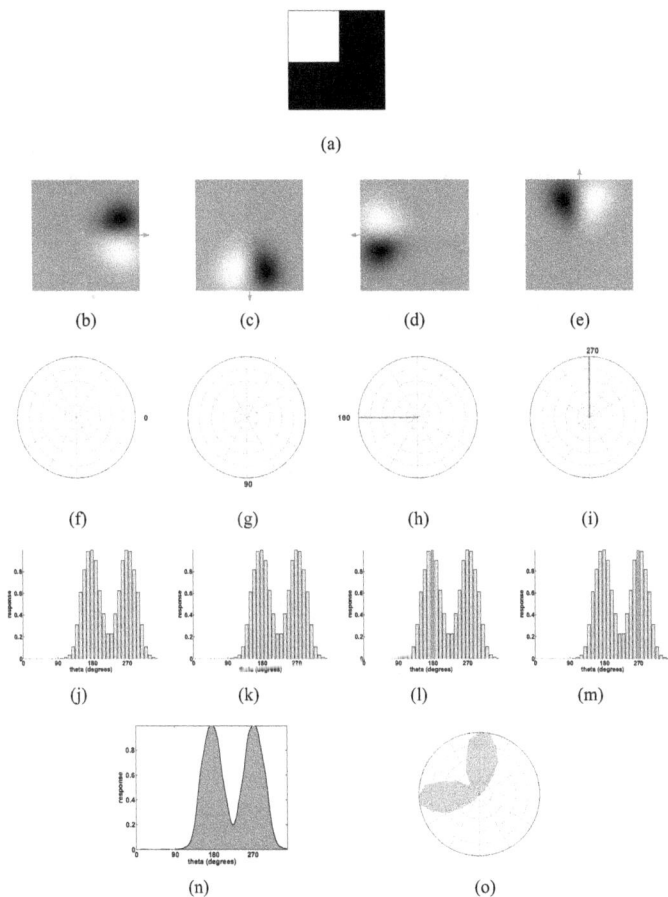

Figure 2.2: (a) sample swatch used to demonstrate how the directional distribution function (DDF) is created. (b-e) odd-phased wedge filters [75] sampled at rotations of 0^0, 90^0, 180^0, and 270^0 respectively denoted by the arrow. (Associated even-phase not shown) (f-i) energy response at corresponding angles in polar form and (j-m) denote the energy superimposed as the darker bar in Cartesian form. (n) Final DDF in Cartesian and (o) in polar form.

$$X = x\cos\left(\theta\right) + y\sin\left(\theta\right)$$

$$Y = -x\sin\left(\theta\right) + y\cos\left(\theta\right)$$

(2.2)

where θ denotes the rotation of the filter with respect to the x-axis, f is the frequency variable, σ_x and σ_y correspond to the variances associated with the 2D Gaussian envelope and P is the phase component that equals zero for even and $\frac{\pi}{2}$ for odd-phased Gabor kernels [21]. Both the even and odd kernels are illustrated for $\theta=0^0$ in Figures 2.1 (a and b) respectively. Despite the increased computational expense compared to the Sobel operator, the majority of research that requires orientation information over a region of interest typically uses some form of a Gabor filter [50, 64]. There are a number of additional advantages of the Gabor, such as its intuitive manipulation using the steerability property [26], as well as being an acceptable approximation of the human visual system [1]; however, the focus of this research is on its accuracy in identifying local direction measurements. One of the issues with the Gabor approach is evident from its response to a corner junction as shown in Figure 2.3a. When a low frequency Gabor ($f = 0.01$) is applied, a diagonal estimation results, as shown in Figure 2.3b. This would seem to be correct perceptually if one viewed the corner swatch as a diagonal black edge with a high degree of aliasing. When a higher frequency Gabor is applied ($f = 1$), the DDF identifies the horizontal and vertical edges in the swatch 2.3c. This emphasizes both the importance of scale and the need for a bank of differently tuned filters to account for patterns with differing spatial frequencies [31]. More importantly, the Gabor outputs a π-periodic response, thus preventing the DDF from distinguishing between the corner as a rotated 'L' junction and the symmetric equivalent (an 'X' junction), which will be referred to as the *symmetric response problem*.

2.1.2   Fourier Method

Another method to construct the DDF is by performing a Fourier transform on the image. For the corner swatch of Figure 2.3a, the collection of Fourier coefficients is formed and illustrated in Figure 2.3d. The DDF is created by summing the coefficients along a line radiating outward from the origin along both θ and $\theta + \pi$ with respect to the x-axis and representing it in polar form as per Fig-

8

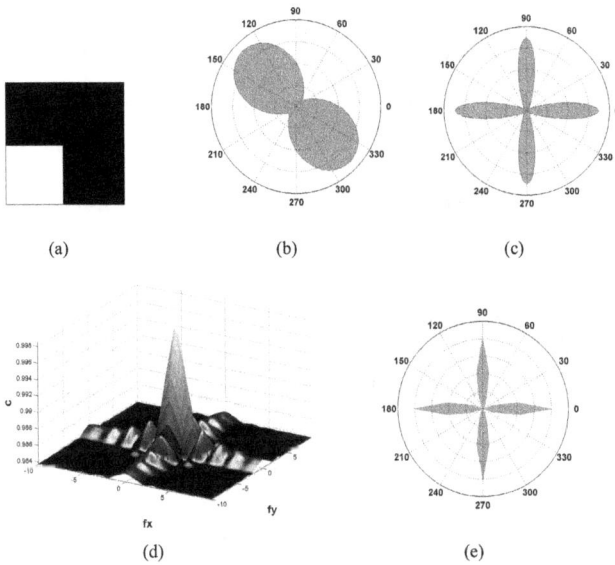

(a)   (b)   (c)

(d)   (e)

Figure 2.3: (a) a corner swatch, (b and c) are the DDFs created using a Gabor at frequencies of $f = 0.01$ and $f = 1$ respectively, (d) the swatch's Fourier spectrum and (e) the Fourier-based DDF.

ure 2.3e [28]. One drawback to this approach is that the Fourier transform does not propagate specific location information into the frequency domain due to the nature of the transformation. This means that proximity-based weighting in the spatial domain, which will be addressed in Section 2.2.1, cannot be applied in the frequency domain. Again, the more fundamental issue is that spectral information is symmetric, hence this approach also suffers from the symmetric response problem.

2.1.3 Asymmetric Convolution Filters

To address this concern, asymmetric quadrature pairs of filters were created. Work by Perona involved a *one-sided* filter that specifically targeted end-points of lines or edges [61]. The asymmetric framework was derived from Equations (2.3 and 2.4). Note that Equation 2.3 takes the form of the first derivative of the Gabor along the x-axis.

$$E\left(x, y, \sigma_x, \sigma_y\right) = G\left(x, y, \sigma_x, \sigma_y\right) \left(\frac{-x}{\sigma_x}\right) \tag{2.3}$$

$$P\left(x, y, \sigma_x, \sigma_y\right) = G\left(x, y, \sigma_x, \sigma_y\right) + E\left(x, y, \sigma_x, \sigma_y\right) \tag{2.4}$$

Although this approach was successful in denoting asymmetric orientations within a sub-region, the filter's DDF also exhibited a small amount of symmetric responses. This was due to the presence of non-zero portions of the kernel spilling out of the asymmetric region. This effect is visualized in Figures 2.1(e-h), where non-zero weights appear in the region where x<0 for kernels at angle $\theta = 0^o$.

Another approach is to use steerable *wedge* filters [75]. In essence, these filters formed a quadrature pair of sector-shaped Gabor filters with polar-based smoothing, as shown in Figures 2.1(i-l). The main advantage of this approach was its ability to delineate multiple directions. Yu designed a slightly different technique known as the rotated averaging wedge method (RAWM) that calculated the average pixel value within a wedge-shaped region, as shown in Figure 2.1(m) [85]. The DDF was constructed by calculating the 1D derivative along the pixel-chain. Early use of information gained from asymmetrically designed kernels was performed using logical-linear operators that expressed a Boolean decision as to the underlying presence of specific gradient structures [34].

10

These asymmetric approaches perform reasonably well on trivial step-edge images, such as those in Figure 2.4. The direction of the diagonal step-edge is identified through the local maxima within the DDFs. However, even with this simulated example, it is noted that the effects of the symmetric portion of the one-sided filter depict an erroneous lobe pointing southwest of the center, as shown in Figure 2.4d. Also, this test case highlights that the choice of parameters is application dependent for the wedge filter, as the angular span was chosen too wide for this test case, thus preventing the proper estimation of a lobe at $\theta = 0^o$. Applying the same approaches to another image with the same gradient locations but a change in the color map, as in Figure 2.4g, it becomes apparent that the respective DDFs have changed significantly. It is the location of the highest contrast edge, which is the black to white step-edge in this example, that biases the respective locations of local maxima in the DDFs. This simple change has most dramatically affected the directional estimates for both the one-sided and wedge filter approaches, as noted by the absence of the diagonal estimate in Figures 2.4(j and k) respectively. It should also be noted that the RAWM worked well for both of these toy examples.

Applying these methods to more challenging T-junction test cases, as in Figure 2.5a, highlights another important issue. This test case exhibits gradient-based contours (edges) that are limited to horizontal and vertical orientations. However, the key is that they do not radiate from the center. As expected, the Gabor and Fourier approaches are accurate in their estimates being horizontal and vertical but are affected by the symmetric response problem. In this scenario, the Fourier approach has the advantage that the DDF is rooted in the spectral, not spatial patterns, thus allowing proper depiction of the vertical pattern even though vertical patterns are not present in the bottom half of the image. Both the one-sided and wedge filter approaches are able to distinguish the horizontally oriented pattern, however, they perform poorly in isolating the vertical pattern. It is the presence of vertical gradient patterns that do not radiate from the center of the image that cause both of these methods to fail. The RAWM performed well on the previous step-edge examples by isolating the correct direcions of the gradient patterns. However, due to the nature of the pixel averaging within the wedge shape, it too exhibits a more erratic DDF.

The cause of the inaccurate portrayal of the underlying horizontal and vertical patterns is twofold. First, there is the sampling issue rooted in the number of an-

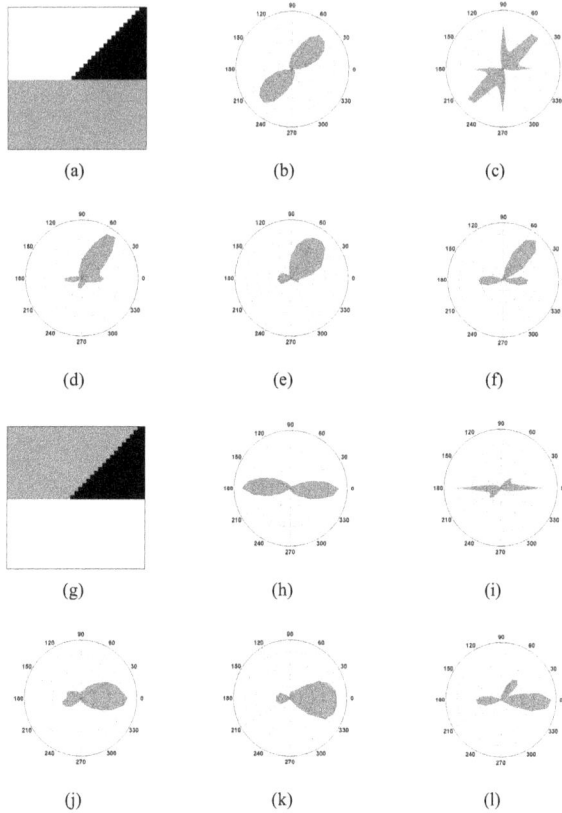

Figure 2.4: (a and g) two slanted 'T'-shaped junctions with different color mappings. (b-f) are the DDFs for the Gabor, Fourier, one-sided, wedge filter and RAWM for (a) respectively, while (h-l) are the DDFs for the Gabor, Fourier, one-sided, wedge filter and RAWM for (g) respectively.

12

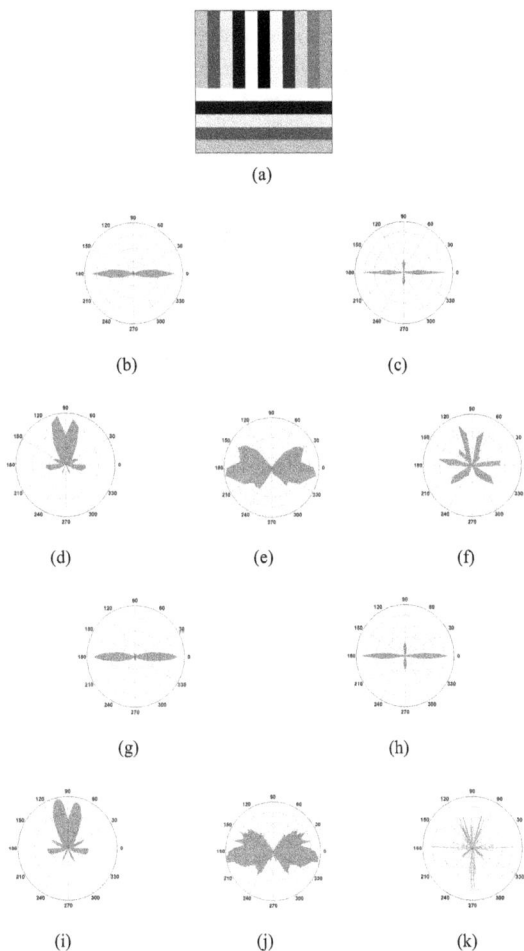

Figure 2.5: (a) Input image and Gabor (b and g), Fourier (c and h), one-sided (d and l), wedge filter (e and j) and RAWM (f and k) DDFs for 36 and 360 angular increments respectively.

13

gular increments. For the DDFs in Figures 2.5(b-f), 36 increments over the range of $[0, 2\pi)$ were used while 360 increments were chosen for the DDfs in Figures 2.5(g-k). The Gabor, Fourier and one-sided filter, which are derived from well-defined equations, have smoothly interpolated versions. The wedge and RWAM, which are dependent on a wedge-shaped kernel parameter, exhibit spurious local maxima in the DDFs to a larger degree than the other methods. The second and more important issue is that the convolution methods are based on template matching. This implies that although the DDF provides a reasonable indicator as to the presence of patterns similar to the kernel, local maxima do not necessarily imply the more general *gradient*-based structures sought [49]. This is expected as the kernels are applied directly to the image data and not to the gradient space. To adapt these approaches to identifying such gradient-based patterns, a large bank of filters tuned to span the spectrum of spatial frequencies must be used to account for all possible cases [31]. Although steerability has been explored in the use of such approaches [61], these methods also have several other parameters to tune. For example, Gabor, one-sided and wedge filters have different frequency parameter choices as well as Gaussian window variables [31, 61, 75]. Also, the wedge filter and RAWM require the selection of radial thresholds to adapt their methods properly [75, 85].

Working directly with gradient information seems a more appropriate approach to identify junctions. Michelet et al. populated the DDF by calculating the average gradient value within an asymmetrically shaped sampling grid [53]. Although this begins to address the problem properly, their method has several variables to tune and more importantly, did not apply any form of local support[4] to add robustness to the measurements.

2.2   Diffusion Techniques

An alternative to creating the DDF using a convolution approach is to propagate gradient data from a pixel location or *node* outward to its corresponding neighbors. This technique has been used under many headings such as voting, data passing, smoothing, regularization, local support, cooperative processes and labeling [32,

---

[4]Local support is the concept of strengthening local estimates that are similar among a large population and weakening those that are apparent in only a few.

37, 44, 52]. In general, however, it falls under the category of *diffusion* [82].[5] This serves several possible functions: it reduces the effects of noise, populates empty nodes amongst sparse data, and adds certainty to those points that 'agree' with their neighbors while lessening those that do not. The primary goal, however, is to strike a balance between the original data and biasing the local behavior.

To clarify both the terminology as well as the motivating factors in many of the diffusion approaches, it is helpful to review briefly the field of perceptual organization.

2.2.1   Perceptual Organization

At the core of diffusion, and indeed many computer vision algorithms, lie Gestalt laws, which are also known as perceptual organization or *percepts* [65, 71, 86]. These are principles that facilitate grouping of data based on hypothesized rules of human visual perception [38, 41, 47]. Although there are several specific sub-groups of these rules, those that appear most often in the vision literature are proximity, similarity, symmetry, closure, continuity, common-fate, parallelism and curvilinearity. *Proximity*, a measure of distance between points, tends to group points that are close to one another as in Figure 2.6a to form four horizontal lines. *Similarity*, as in Figure 2.6b, groups like-points along four vertical lines. In Figure 2.6c, we tend to perceive two overlapping curves: a sine-like wave and a diagonal line, which falls under *continuity*, while a circle is perceived using *closure* in Figure 2.6d. When dealing with line segments, we perceive a degree of colinearity, parallelism and co-termination in Figures 2.6(e-g) respectively. Many of these concepts are not mutually exclusive. For example, co-termination may be explained as proximity of end-points of the lines. *Common fate*, where features that follow similar motion paths are clustered, could be described as a measure of parallelism through the grouping of spatio-temporal based parallel contours as noted by Korimilli and Sarkar [42].

An example in computer vision applications that enforces percepts is a simple Gaussian smoothing operator that diffuses pixel data based on the neighboring pixel's proximity to the center. The anisotropic diffusion methods, which are

---

[5]Diffusion traditionally has two definitions. The first refers to the solution of a partial differential equation given initial boundary conditions, while the second provides a more general term for the iterative updating of information from data passing. Both definitions have significant overlap; however, throughout this literature the second definition will be used.

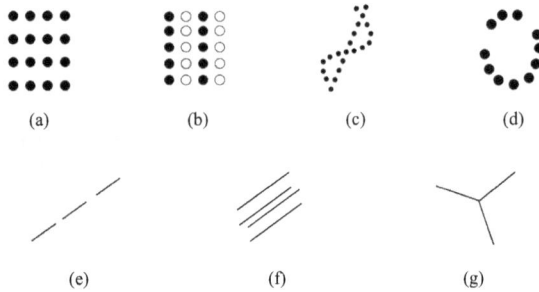

Figure 2.6: Examples of Gestalt laws of perception. (a) proximity, (b) similarity, (c) continuity, (d) closure, (e) colinearity, (f) parallelism and (g) co-termination.

detailed in the Section 2.2.2, attempt to modify local data to become more *similar* to the perceived gradient direction by spreading data along the gradient, weighted by its *proximity* to the center pixel. There are also some percept-based side effects to anisotropic diffusion that pertain to *closure* and *continuity* where local edges are separated by a gap.

Implementing perceptual organization in a computer vision algorithm can take many forms such as a Bayesian framework or a rule-based system [42, 54, 71]; however, the focus of this research is to apply these concepts to the diffusion architecture [8]. Guy and Medioni implemented a diffusion-type approach using percepts through specialized *extension fields* that highlighted both straight-line regions as well as end-point locations [29]. Their method converted an initial collection of points into a vector field and subsequently grouped this data using the percepts of curvilinearity, proximity and constancy of curvature. This method highlighted the spatial locations of junctions and contours, as well as illusionary contours and became the precursor for research into *tensor voting*, which will be detailed in Section 2.2.4.

In order to make use of the principles of perceptual organization, the *form* that the data takes must first be addressed. In the domain of junction analysis, this implies the choice of gradient representation.

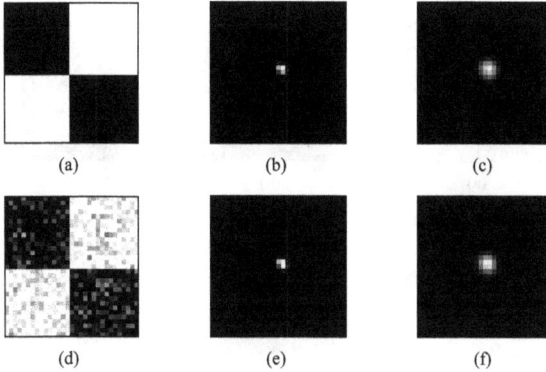

(a)	(b)	(c)
(d)	(e)	(f)

Figure 2.7: Using Equation 2.5 against (a) 'checker' swatch of 31x31, (b and c) results for differential scale 15 and 31 respectively, which correspond to the half and full size of the swatch. (d) the same checker swatch with 50% additive Gaussian noise, (e and f) results using differential scales 15 and 31 respectively.

2.2.2 Structure Tensors

There are many ways to detect junctions based on differential information. For example, Salden et al. used fourth-order derivatives to isolate junction locations via the discriminant of the truncated Taylor expansion [69]. A fourth-order differential invariant version of this is outlined in Equation 2.5 [46]:

$$
\begin{aligned}
D_4\left(I\left(x,y\right)\right) = &-\left(I_{x^4}I_{y^4} - 4I_{x^3y}I_{xy^3} + 3I_{x^2y^2}^2\right)^3 \\
&+27\left[I_{x^4}\left(I_{x^2y^2}I_{y^4} - I_{xy^3}^2\right) - I_{x^3y}\left(I_{x^3y}I_{y^4} - I_{x^2y^2}I_{xy^3}\right)\right. \\
&\left.+I_{x^2y^2}\left(I_{x^3y}I_{xy^3} - I_{x^2y^2}^2\right)\right]^2
\end{aligned}
\tag{2.5}
$$

where I_p denotes the partial derivative of image I along axis p. This process was shown to work well for a select set of image conditions, specifically black and white images, and was robust to additive Gaussian noise as well, as illustrated in Figure 2.7.

The drawback to using fourth-order derivative information is that a large pixel area must be used to calculate such data. This issue is more prominent in the presence of three or more color values in the input image. For example, in Figure 2.8,

17

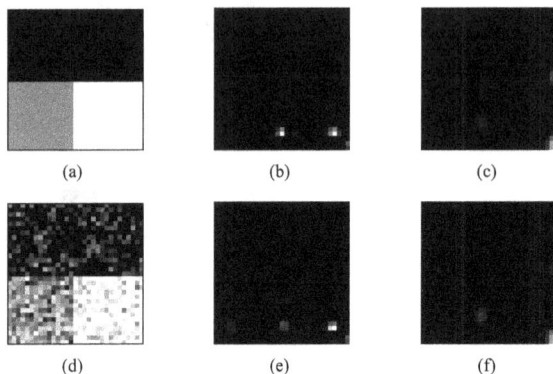

(a)   (b)   (c)

(d)   (e)   (f)

Figure 2.8: Using Equation 2.5 against (a) three-toned T-junction swatch of 31x31, (b and c) results for differential scale 15 and 31 respectively, which correspond to the half and full size of the swatch. (d) the same three-toned T-junction swatch with 50% additive Gaussian noise, (e and f) results using differential scales 15 and 31 respectively.

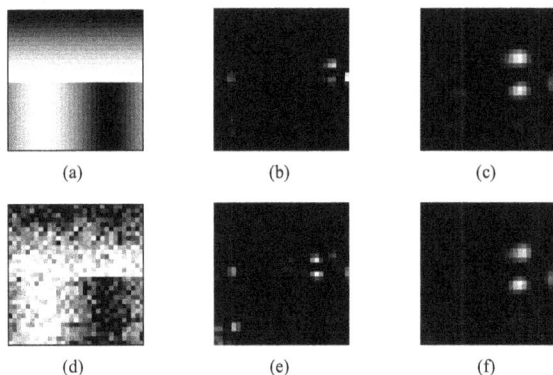

(a)   (b)   (c)

(d)   (e)   (f)

Figure 2.9: Using Equation 2.5 against (a) T-junction swatch with constant spatial frequency with dimensions 31x31, (b and c) results for differential scale 15 and 31 respectively, which correspond to the half and full size of the swatch. (d) the same swatch having constant spatial frequency with 50% additive Gaussian noise, (e and f) results using differential scales 15 and 31 respectively.

even though the junction occurs between the white, gray and black regions, this approach tends to smooth over junction locations in using fourth-order derivative information. In Figure 2.9, the fourth-order invariant equation centers about the white to black transition region; however, is unable to discern the vertical white bar intersecting with the horizontal white bar in the left of the image. There is also the issue of choosing among many possible scales from which to calculate the partial derivatives, as in Figures 2.8 and 2.9. For these reasons, first-order gradient information will be focused on in this thesis. Two such forms are directional derivatives and structure tensors.[6] Although the former may be sufficient for some applications to represent the gradient, the latter are far more versatile and encode more detailed information in the form of coherence [35, 43]. For example, if the gradient magnitude is zero, the distinction as to whether the image data originated from a region depicting isointensity versus an isotropic pattern cannot be determined with the directional derivative. However, this distinction *can* be made by performing the eigen-decomposition of the symmetric structure tensor S, Equation 2.6, and noting the relationship between the resulting eigenvalues [57]. The structure tensor is useful as when applying a Gaussian smoothing operator element-by-element, local shifting of edge information in the image is minimized. Furthermore, the cancellations of opposing gradient polarity directions are prevented when structure tensors are summed [17].

$$ S = \begin{bmatrix} I_x^2 & I_x I_y & I_x I_t \\ I_x I_y & I_y^2 & I_y I_t \\ I_x I_t & I_y I_t & I_t^2 \end{bmatrix} \tag{2.6} $$

where $I = I(x, y, t)$ and I_p is the partial derivative of I along dimension p. The eigen-decomposition of the structure tensor representation allows a concise breakdown of the coherence of the gradient measure as well as a pseudo basis description of the underlying structure type where $\lambda_1 \geq \lambda_2 \geq \lambda_3 \geq 0$.

---

[6]A *tensor* is a generic term given to a quantity that is expressed as a multi-dimensional array. The rank of a tensor is the number of indices required to describe the quantity. For example, a vector is a tensor of rank one where it may be expressed as $v_i = (v_1, v_2, ... v_n)$ while a two-dimensional matrix is a tensor of rank two as the elements can be described by two subscript indices as m_{ij}. A scalar is a tensor of rank zero.

19

$$S = (\lambda_1 - \lambda_2)\, \vec{e}_1 \vec{e}_1^T + (\lambda_2 - \lambda_3)\left(\vec{e}_1 \vec{e}_1^T + \vec{e}_2 \vec{e}_2^T\right) +$$
$$\lambda_3 \left(\vec{e}_1 \vec{e}_1^T + \vec{e}_2 \vec{e}_2^T + \vec{e}_3 \vec{e}_3^T\right) \tag{2.7}$$

where $(\vec{e}_1, \vec{e}_2, \vec{e}_3)$ and $(\lambda_1, \lambda_2, \lambda_3)$ are the eigenvectors and eigenvalues of the structure tensor S respectively. In the 2D image domain, the eigenvector associated with the largest eigenvalue is directed perpendicular to the gradient edge while the second eigenvector is tangent to the edge. The eigenvalues themselves indicate the underlying saliency of the gradient structure along their associated eigenvector directions. As noted by several authors [35, 52, 82], the difference between λ_1 and λ_2 indicates the *coherence* of the gradient information in the local region. Tschumperlé and Deriche expressed coherence using Equation 2.8 [82], while Jähne chose to express coherence as the ratio of the difference and its sum, also known as the *mean gradient measure*, denoted by Equation 2.9 [35].

$$\varsigma = \sqrt{\lambda_1 - \lambda_2} \tag{2.8}$$

$$\varsigma = \begin{cases} \left(\frac{\lambda_1 - \lambda_2}{\lambda_1 + \lambda_2}\right)^2 & \text{if } (\lambda_1 + \lambda_2) > 0 \\ 0 & \text{otherwise} \end{cases} \tag{2.9}$$

Using Equation 2.9 provides a measure to distinguish between regions of isointensity and isotropic structure in the presence of zero gradient magnitude [35]. For example, the step-edge in Figure 2.10a would give rise to a high gradient magnitude along the horizontal orientation. The distinction between the black circle and the isointensity regions, Figure 2.10(b and c) respectively, could not be made based solely on gradient magnitude as neither reveal a preferred, or maximal gradient direction estimation. By using the coherence measure, the black circle is properly distinguished by coherence lesser than that of the isointensity region.

Several algorithms that rely on the identification of locations based on the presence of two underlying gradient features such as corner detectors or salient point locations [24, 30, 67, 81] quantify such features using the eigenvalues extracted from the gradient structure tensor form [39].

20

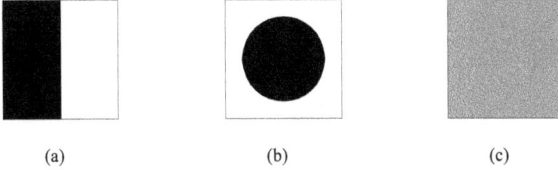

(a)   (b)   (c)

Figure 2.10: The case for a coherence measure: (a) step-edge with a single gradient orientation possible, (b) isotropic gradient pattern where there is no single, maximal gradient orientation and (c) a monochromatic region where the gradient magnitude and coherence equals zero.

The interpretation of eigenvalues and eigenvectors can also be visualized as a 3D ellipse in the 3D domain [52], as in Figure 2.11. This is accomplished by representing the differences between pairs of eigenvalues as being relative to the elliptical radii. These difference values in turn indicate the underlying structural element. For example, if the value of $(\lambda_1 - \lambda_2) \gg 0$, this depicts a local surface element (surfel) where $\vec{e}_1$ denotes the normal to that surface and is referred to as the *stick tensor* [52,57]. A local curve element (curvel) is identified as $(\lambda_2 - \lambda_3) \gg 0$ where $\vec{e}_3$ denotes the tangent along the curve. If $\lambda_3 \gg 0$ then isotropic behavior is present and denoted by a *ball tensor*. The eigenvalues and their respective eigenvectors allow a rich depiction of local structure as well as provide an architecture that is generalizable to higher dimensions [43,57].

2.2.3 Anisotropic Diffusion

The diffusion framework is well suited to the task of finding a balance between maintaining the original information while biasing the local model. The former is facilitated through the data consistency term while the latter uses a diffusion or regularization term, defined in Equation 2.10.

$$E\left(I\right) = \int_{\Omega} \left[\frac{\alpha}{2} \left(I - I_o\right)^2 + \phi\left(\|\nabla I\|\right) \right] \partial\Omega \qquad (2.10)$$

where the ϕ-function represents the diffusion term with respect to the image gradient ∇I, α is the learning term that balances the data consistency versus the amount of regularization desired in the output image I and I_o is the original data.

21

(a)

(b)

(c)

(d)

Figure 2.11: (a) gradient structure tensor representation expressed in elliptical form, with the three basic forms denoting (b) a surface element (surfel), (c) curve element (curvel) and (d) an isotropic region [52].

Ω is the domain over which the data is integrated, such as the spatial domain when applied to images [82].

Diffusion is best described using political election terminology. At its core, it spreads information from a node, which will be referred to as the *voter*, to its neighboring nodes, or *receivers*. The *ballot*, the information itself that is propagated, is sent from the voters to the receivers where it is collected and tallied. The results of this election form the new ballot that will be used in the next iteration of voting. It is both the form of the ballot as well as the method by which the ballots are tallied that distinguishes the various diffusion approaches. A typical strategy is to apply a weighting kernel to bias ballots that conform with a single or multiple percepts, such as proximity or similarity, as well as to create a ballot field that is a function of the voter's ballot itself. For example, with isotropic diffusion the weighting kernel is based solely on relative proximity, where those receivers closer to the voter collect a stronger ballot than those further away, as illustrated in Figure 2.12a. The ballot field simply repeats the ballot information from the voter to all of the receivers. For example, if the initial information is a horizontal orientation, as it is in the examples illustrated in Figure 2.12, the resulting ballot field will be a mask of horizontal orientations, such as that shown in Figure 2.12b. Isotropic diffusion is a commonly applied diffusion technique that reduces the effects of noise at the expense of high gradient edge information. To retain the gradient data, anisotropic diffusion was proposed to constrain the weighting kernel to smooth less in regions of high gradient information, along with various approaches that also have an orientational quality to smooth *along* rather than *across* edges [63, 83]. Although several different terms refer to a gradient-conditioned smoothing approach such as bilateral filtering [79] and adaptive smoothing [68], they are based on the same fundamentals [5]. Using Euler-Lagrange equations, Equation 2.10 can be rewritten as:

$$\frac{\partial I}{\partial t} = \alpha \left(I - I_o \right) + div \left(\frac{\phi \left(\|\nabla I\| \right)}{\|\nabla I\|} \nabla I \right) \qquad (2.11)$$

where *div* is the divergence. Equation 2.11 can be further decomposed to:

$$\frac{\partial I}{\partial t} = \alpha \left(I - I_o \right) + c_\eta I_{\eta\eta} + c_\xi I_{\xi\xi} \qquad (2.12)$$

23

$$c_\eta = \phi'' \left(\|\nabla I\| \right), c_\xi = \frac{\phi' \left(\|\nabla I\| \right)}{\|\nabla I\|} \qquad (2.13)$$

This framework implies that the data is smoothed with a weighting of c_η along the direction $I_{\eta\eta}$, which corresponds to the direction orthogonal to the gradient edge and c_ξ is the smoothing weight along the tangent direction [82]. It can now be seen how the vectors $I_{\eta\eta}$ and $I_{\xi\xi}$ correspond to the eigenvectors as well as the eigenvalues and the c variables described in the previous section. The goal of anisotropic diffusion is to diffuse isotropically in the presence of low gradient magnitudes ($c_\eta \approx c_\xi$) while biasing *along* rather than *across* high gradient magnitudes ($c_\eta \ll c_\xi$). The choice of ϕ-function distinguishes between the different anisotropic diffusion. For example, Perona and Malik implemented a ϕ-function, sometimes referred to as the *conductance equation*, using:

$$\phi' \left(\|\nabla I\| \right) = e^{-\left(\left(\|\nabla I\|/\beta \right)^2 \right)} \qquad (2.14)$$

where β is a constant [63]. Further research into the conductance equation showed that for some gradient inputs, it became ill-posed [18]. Another version was later proposed by Monteil and Beghdadi of the form:

$$\phi' \left(\|\nabla I\| \right) = \frac{1}{2} \left[\tanh \left(\gamma \left(\beta - \|\nabla I\| \right) \right) + 1 \right] \qquad (2.15)$$

where γ determines the slope of the gradient gray value or transition region, in which diffusion is performed [55]. By reformulating the conductance equation in such a manner, the transition region remains constant for different values of β. Later research addressed the *pinhole effect*[7] by implementing a set of rules to detect such a phenomenon [55]. Weickert implemented a *diffusion tensor* created from eigenvalues related to c_η and c_ξ with eigenvectors along $I_{\eta\eta}$ and $I_{\xi\xi}$ to perform anisotropic diffusion [83]. Other anisotropic diffusion methods exist that have similar but distinct ϕ-functions [13, 40, 70, 82]. Further improvements were obtained by adding robustness to the conductance equation [12], as well as designing an architecture for orientation estimates and vector-valued images [62,82]. Al-

---

[7]Pinhole Effect: When a pixel of intermediate intensity, gray for example, is positioned along a strong transition region, such as a black to white step-edge [55].

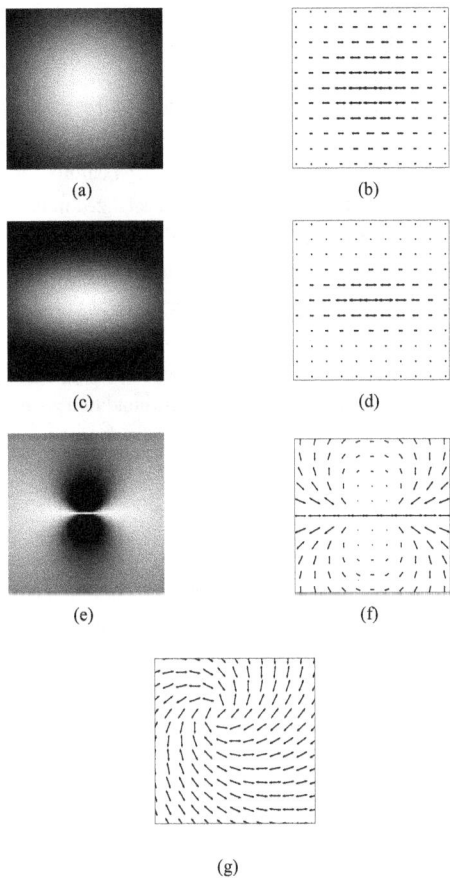

Figure 2.12: Weighting kernels and associated weighted directional bins for a horizontal orientation at the center. (a and b) the isotropic case, (c and d) anisotropic case, (e and f) tensor voting [52], (g) the right-helicoid model for relaxation labeling using $\kappa_N = 0.7$ and $\kappa_T = 0.9$ [9].

though some approach the problem by enhancing blurred information rather than strictly smoothing based on gradient values [84], the goal remains the same: to enhance certain image features while reducing others. A generalized anisotropic weighting kernel in the form of a 2D Gaussian where $\sigma_y = \frac{1}{2}\sigma_x$ oriented along the x-axis is shown in Figure 2.12c.

Typical anisotropic diffusion methods are insufficient for identifying junctions as they diffuse information based solely on proximity and the original gradient orientation. Another approach, *orientation diffusion* enforces the periodic nature of symmetric gradient information through a specialized influence function [62]. Several other methods refer to direction-based diffusion in the context of gradient polarity direction to bolster pixel-based feature points or in the framework of color enhancement [48, 76]. However, the focus of this thesis is on a phase-*independent* description of the gradient structure. This implies the need for an algorithm that would add confidence to local structures by diffusing not only gradient information from the center node, but also conditioned on other structurally based percepts.

2.2.4   Tensor Voting

Using the structure tensor representation, tensor voting diffuses local gradient-based structural information with an emphasis on several percepts [52, 57]. In addition, the notion of pair-wise geometric characteristics is included through the calculation of curvature in the decay function, DF. Data passing in the form of normal orientations to contours between pairs of points is facilitated through a *voting field*, depicted in Figure 2.12f. The voting field itself is based on Equation 2.16:

$$DF\left(s, \kappa, \sigma\right) = e^{-\left(\frac{s^2 + c\kappa^2}{\sigma^2}\right)} \tag{2.16}$$

where s denotes the arc length formed from the common osculating circle between the pair of tangent orientations, κ the curvature and σ the scale of the voting field. The parameter c biases toward lines rather than curves.

As previously discussed in Section 2.2.2, the ballots are weighted by the eigenvalues (saliencies) associated with their voting field shapes. The three dimensional, first-order stick, plate and ball voting field are defined as per Equations

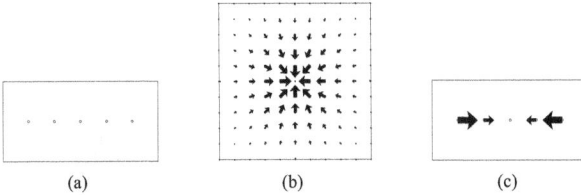

(a)   (b)   (c)

Figure 2.13: (a) An initial set of points with no initial gradient estimate, (b) the first-order ball voting field that is applied at each point, (c) the equivalent summation of the vectors collected at each of these points, which denotes both termination (by the magnitude) and polarity (by the direction) [80].

(2.17-2.19) [80].

$$F_S\left(\rho, \theta\right) = DF\left(s, \kappa, \sigma\right) \begin{bmatrix} -\cos\left(2\theta\right) \\ -\sin\left(2\theta\right) \end{bmatrix} \qquad (2.17)$$

$$F_P\left(\rho, \theta\right) = \int_0^{\pi} R_{\theta\phi\gamma}^{-1} F_S\left(R_{\theta\phi\gamma} P\right) R_{\theta\phi\gamma}^T d\gamma \,|_{\theta=\phi=0} \qquad (2.18)$$

$$F_D\left(P\right) = \int_0^{\pi}\int_0^{\pi} R_{\theta\psi\gamma}^{-1} F_{\mathcal{E}}\left(R_{\theta\phi\gamma} P\right) R_{\theta\psi}^T{}_, d\theta d\gamma \,|_{\theta=0} \qquad (2.19)$$

where ρ is the spherical radius, θ, ϕ, γ are rotation angles about x, y, z axes respectively at point P, and R is the rotation matrix. The first-order ball-voting field F_B serves to identify both polarity and termination of contours. For example, consider the sparse set of five points in Figure 2.13a. If the first-order ball voting field, depicted in Figure 2.13b, distributed single vector ballots to each of the neighboring points, the vector summation at each of those points would result in Figure 2.13c. The single vector representation at each node uses the vector's magnitude and direction to depict the *termination* and *polarity* respectively at that point. Termination is a measurement that represents the certainty that a particular point is an end-point to a contour while polarity offers the estimated direction to the next node on a common contour [80].

The second-order voting fields propagate the local structure of the underlying pattern. The final collection of ballots is calculated through a tensor summation of

27

the contributing voters within the neighborhood of the receiver, weighted by the individual saliencies as per Equation 2.20:

$$G(P_i) = \sum_{j=1}^{\Omega} \Big[(\lambda_1 - \lambda_2)_j \, F_S \, (P_{ij}, \vec{e}_{1j}) \\ + (\lambda_2 - \lambda_3)_j \, F_P \, (P_{ij}, \vec{e}_1) + \lambda_3 F_B \, (P_{ij}) \Big] \tag{2.20}$$

where P_{ij} denotes the relative position between point i and j from the neighborhood Ω. The final tensor depicts structural information with associated saliency measures [52, 57]. This diffusion or voting approach improves upon the standard anisotropic diffusion methods as it is able to incorporate similarity between curvatures as well as proximity into the voting field. This results in a symmetric representation capable of inferring local curve and surface structure [52]. It also allows for easy generalization to create a dense data field from sparse information.

One of the difficulties with this approach is in the proper selection of scale to use in applying the voting fields. One popular technique addresses this problem by combining information over multiple scales [19, 45], yielding satisfactory results. However, thresholds and other constraints must be applied to dictate the manner in which the features are allowed to vary between resolution levels. Elder and Zucker addressed this issue by calculating a minimum reliable scale using the gradient information in conjunction with the sensor noise in an attempt to identify the most pertinent contours in a scene [23].

Tensor voting identifies junctions as those nodes that exhibit isotropic (ball) structure surrounded by neighbors with an anisotropic structure [80]. This approach is satisfactory for the identification of junctions with initially sparse and noisy data. However, it is inappropriate when the data is initially dense, such as with pixel-based gradient information from an image where each node potentially has a strong initial estimate. Furthermore, identifying junctions as locations of lesser certainty surrounded by those of greater certainty is far too general to isolate gradient-based junctions in a densely populated space. Finally, as with the anisotropic diffusion, in particular Perona's orientation diffusion method [62], tensor voting has no mechanism by which to maintain singularities explicitly as the nodes become too heavily influenced by their neighbors. Diffusion methods average incoming ballots into a *single* representational structure tensor at the receiver. Thus, they are unable to represent non-orthogonal orientational estimates

28

as junctions require.

2.2.5   Relaxation Labeling

Relaxation labeling allows *multiple* labels, or in this case, orientation estimates, at a node rather than expressing it as a single structure tensor [32]. The framework itself is similar to tensor voting in that information is diffused based on proximity, although instead of a Gaussian, a binary window is used in some implementations [60]. However, the focus is placed on increasing local support based on the compatibility between two nodes. The only pair-wise diffusion feature of tensor voting is inherent in the curvature variable of the decay function.[8] Relaxation labeling allows for the integration of many different co-nodal properties. In other words, whereas the previous diffusion approaches propagate data based *solely* on the voter, relaxation labeling focuses on the relationship *between* the voter and the receiver.

This is performed by creating a *compatibility function* r_{ij} that provides a measure of consistency between nodes i and j. Along with the local confidence in each label for all of the nodes in the system, the *contextual support* can be calculated as per Equation 2.21:

$$s_i\left(\lambda\right) = \sum_{j=1}^{\Omega}\sum_{\lambda'=1}^{\Lambda} r_{ij}\left(\lambda,\lambda'\right)p_j\left(\lambda'\right) \tag{2.21}$$

where $p_j(\lambda)$ denotes the probability of label λ at node j, Ω is the local spatial neighborhood for i and Λ is the set of labels [60]. Contextual support represents how well a particular label λ at node i agrees with the estimates of its neighbors. The probabilities are updated iteratively using Equation 2.22:

$$p_i^{t+1}\left(\lambda\right) \leftarrow \Pi_{\mathrm{K}}\left[p_i^t\left(\lambda\right) + \delta s_i^t\left(\lambda\right)\right] \tag{2.22}$$

where δ is the update coefficient and Π_{K} is a projection operator that bounds the possible assignment of probabilities between zero and one [9].

The choice of compatibility function differentiates the existing relaxation la-

---

[8]More recent literature attempts to modify the tensor voting fields after local curvature is estimated to sign [77].

beling implementations. For example, using a measure of *co-circularity* tends to strengthen structural estimates that depict tangents among a common circle [60]. This approach is ideal for grouping vectors or tensors that depict local tangents to sparse underlying contours. The co-circularity approach is similar to the stick voting field of tensor voting in that local curvature dictates how information is passed from node to node. The compatibility function based on co-circularity takes the form of Equation 2.23:

$$r_{ij}^{kk'} (\lambda, \lambda') = c_{ij} (\lambda, \lambda') E_{ij} K_{ij}^{k} (\lambda, \lambda') C_{ij}^{kk'} (\lambda, \lambda') l (\lambda') \qquad (2.23)$$

where (k, k') are the curvature classes,[9] c_{ij} determines the co-circularity coefficient and E_{ij} and K_{ij}^{k} dictate the outer boundary of the binary region-of-influence (ROI) map. $C_{ij}^{kk'}$ calculates the *curvature consistency* between two curvature classes such that given two labels and two curvature classes, the relationship is strengthened based on the mutual overlap [60].

Another example of a compatibility function uses the right-helicoid, as per Equation 2.24, as its model can handle denser layouts of data [9]. This particular approach enforces local structure within *texture flows* where there is a number of parallel curves in the input. The general relaxation labeling abstraction is modified for ease of computation, and the nodes are set in 5D space with $i = (x, y, \theta, \kappa_T, \kappa_N)$ where θ is the local gradient orientation, and κ_T and κ_N represent the tangential and normal curvature values respectively.

$$\theta (x, y) = \tan^{-1} \left(\frac{\kappa_T x + \kappa_N y}{1 + \kappa_N x - \kappa_T y} \right) \qquad (2.24)$$

The compatibility function is based on node i and j, along with their respective curvature values, being a part of the same right-helicoid, which is illustrated in Figure 2.12g. This implementation allows for slowly-varying dominant orientation characterized by local parallelism [9]. Other forms of compatibility functions have been implemented, including a 3D version that measures *co-helicity*, which examines both the curvature and torsion [72].

There are several differences between the tensor voting and relaxation label-

---

[9]The exact curvature measures are discretized and grouped into seven bands of curvatures. It is these bands that are used as the curvature classes.

ing approaches. For example, tensor voting is less computationally expensive as it performs only a single iteration at a fixed scale.[10] It also has less memory requirements per node as the local structure is stored in a single tensor representation. Most of the earlier work defined its proximity parameter as arc-length [52, 80]; however, more recent work uses Euclidean distance to reduce computational complexity [58]. In contrast, relaxation labeling addresses the diffusion of data in an iterative manner. Although this has greater computational requirements, by enforcing local support of the gradient structures over several iterations, this approach is less sensitive to the initial scale. By allowing multiple estimates at each node, relaxation labeling is more memory intensive but allows for a richer structural description.

Some of the challenges of the implemented relaxation labeling approaches are that they do not account for the gradient *magnitude* of the central node or that of its neighboring nodes. Furthermore, the proximity is modeled on a binary rather than a Gaussian window, although it is an iterative approach [60]. Even though this approach can disambiguate between multiple orientations, its initial data is still based on symmetric information from the structure tensors, thus preventing the proper distinction between *directions* of gradient structure. This implies that even with the potential for multiple orientational representations at each node, it still suffers from the symmetric response problem. A method is required that transforms the structure tensor into a ballot based on *direction*, not orientation, to disambiguate between asymmetric junctions in order to represent the data in a more powerful depiction.

---

[10]More recent work has investigated a multi-scale version of this algorithm [80].

Chapter 3

Asymmetric Tensor Diffusion

The problem with the previous diffusion methods is that they seed their processes *directly* with symmetric information derived from the structure tensor. As orientation is π-periodic or *symmetric*, the output from these diffusion techniques will also be symmetric. What is required is a logical transformation of orientation data into appropriate *directional* components. This would allow the data to diffuse in a non-π-periodic manner thus enabling the proper representation of asymmetric junctions. This work proposes such a technique referred to as *asymmetric tensor diffusion* (ATD) that transforms the structure tensor's orientation data into a directional voting field [3]. This field is applied at each node and the ballots are collected into their respective neighboring nodes. Next, the ballots are combined to form a directional distribution function (DDF) that is used to seed a secondary diffusion stage. Within this stage of processing, several different approaches are explored that enhance the local support of asymmetric structures. Sections 3.1 and 3.2 explain each of these stages in further detail.

3.1 Stage One: Directional Voting Field

The process of transforming a structure tensor into a directional voting field begins by extracting its key features. Given a structure tensor representation of gradient information the orientation and magnitude are calculated as per Equations (3.2 and 3.3):

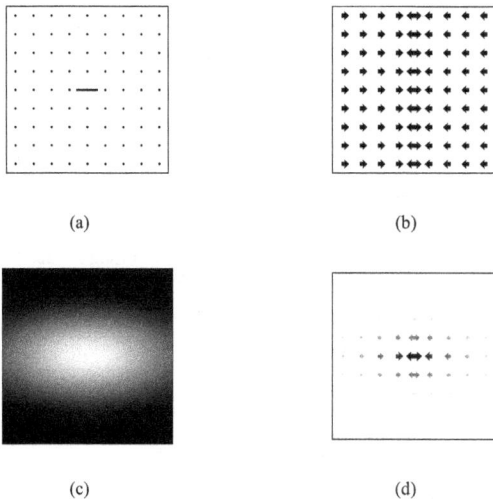

(a)

(b)

(c)

(d)

Figure 3.1: (a) an input of a horizontally oriented structure tensor with $\varsigma = 1$ (b) resulting directional bin field B_{ij} from (a). The double-headed vectors denote directional ambiguity (orientation). (c) the directional bin field is then combined with the ballot weighting function Λ_{ij}, (d) the voting field formed by combining (b and c).

$$S = \begin{bmatrix} I_x^2 & I_x I_y \\ I_x I_y & I_y^2 \end{bmatrix} \qquad (3.1)$$

$$\theta = orientation\,(\vec{e}_1) \qquad (3.2)$$

$$|S| = (\lambda_1 - \lambda_2) \qquad (3.3)$$

where $(\vec{e}_1, \vec{e}_2)$ and (λ_1, λ_2) represent the eigenvectors and eigenvalues from S respectively. The coherence ς is calculated as well using Equation 2.9. The function *orientation* returns the equivalent angle of $\vec{e}_1$ with respect to the x-axis ranging between $[0, 2\pi)$.

33

Next, an *inward* facing[1], directional bin field is constructed. This represents the initial ballot bins and the spatial locations of their corresponding receivers. This concept is best described using the analogy of a political election. As reviewed in Chapter 2, the previous diffusion methods send ballots from a voter to its receivers. The former serves as the location from which data is distributed while the latter is akin to spatially dependent voting station. Rather than sending ballots in the form of orientation alone, directional ballots are used in the proposed implementation. This allows for the creation of asymmetric DDFs. The directional bin field specified by a direction, B_{ij} and magnitude, Ψ_{ij} is calculated as follows:

$$B_{ij}\left(\theta_i, \varepsilon\right) = \begin{cases} \theta_i + \varepsilon\pi & \langle\theta_i - \varphi_{ij}\rangle \leq \frac{\pi}{2} \\ \theta_i + \left(\varepsilon + 1\right)\pi & \text{otherwise} \end{cases} \qquad (3.4)$$

$$\Psi_{ij}\left(\varepsilon\right) = \begin{cases} 1 & |x_{ij}| \leq \frac{1}{2}\tau \\ \varepsilon & \text{otherwise} \end{cases} \qquad (3.5)$$

where τ is the minimum distance between nodes[2] and φ_{ij} denotes the angle from voter i to receiver j with respect to the x-axis. The function of Ψ is to distinguish between single and double ballot locations where the latter is assigned to points of orientational ambiguity. The role of ε, which is either one or zero, is to distinguish between the double and single ballots. This is illustrated in Figure 3.1b as double- and single-headed arrows along the perpendicular axis within the directional bin field. The $\langle...\rangle$ notation returns the angular span between the two angles, taking into account π-periodicity and ranging between $[0, \pi)$. The subscript ij implies the relative location between node i and j, where $B_{ij}\left(\theta_i, \varepsilon\right)$ is equivalent to $B\left(x_{ij}, y_{ij}, \theta_i, \varepsilon\right)$.

This process is illustrated for a horizontally oriented structure tensor in Figure 3.1a. The associated directional bin field, as shown in Figure 3.1b, forms a collection of vectors that are aligned horizontally to correspond with the input. It should be noted that the field consists of parallel vectors that point inward toward the y-axis and not toward the origin. This is in contrast to previous methods that direct the vectors as a function of relative curvature [52, 60]. Inward parallel bal-

---

[1]Inward, for stage one, is defined as pointing toward the axis *normal* to the original orientation value.

[2]The parameter τ is one for an evenly-spaced grid.

lots are chosen instead to reduce initial biasing of the orientation data at an early stage of processing [46]. Further interpolation between the ballots is performed in the second stage of this process.

Since the original data is in orientation form, meaning that it is initially symmetric, the directional bin field reflects this in the voting field as *two* ballots at the center of the voting field. Finally, to account for those locations perpendicular to the originally symmetric information, the ballot pair at the center is replicated along the perpendicular axis (the y-axis in this example).

In brief, the voting field is summarized as follows. Given a single structure tensor at voter i, both the orientation θ_i and magnitude $|S_i|$ are derived as per Equations (3.2,3.3). At each receiver j there are N non-overlapping directional bins spanning $[0, 2\pi)$. These bins collect ballots in a histogramming manner. The directional bin field maps which bin at j is incremented by the ballot sent from i. The strength of each ballot sent from voter i to receiver j is then weighting by an anisotropic map, known as the region-of-influence (ROI) function, Λ_{ij}, which is aligned with the orientation of the original data. The ROI is calculated as follows:

$$\Lambda_{ij}\left(\theta_i, \varepsilon\right) = G_{ij}\left(0, \sigma_x\right) \Psi_{ij}\left(\theta_i, \varepsilon\right) R\left(\theta_i\right) \tag{3.6}$$

where Λ_{ij} is the ballot weight sent from voter i to receiver j and $R(\theta_i)$ is the rotation matrix. G is a 2D Gaussian, normalized to sum to one, with zero mean and $\sigma_y = q\sigma_x$ where q is the sigma ratio ($q = \frac{1}{2}$ in Figure 3.1c). This allows the first stage of the ATD to mimic the directional biasing of anisotropic diffusion. The ROI is combined with the directional bin field to form the final voting field, as shown in Figure 3.1d. Each ballot is illustrated as a vector pointing in the direction corresponding to the bin in which it is collected at the receiver, while the vector magnitude reflects the strength of the ballot.

Rather than summing into a single value as do several of the methods reviewed in Chapter 2, a histogram of N directional bins is used to collect the ballots as per Equation 3.7. This representation allows for multiple directional estimates at each node, which is key to distinguishing asymmetric junction structures.

$$DDF_j\left(\vartheta\right) = \sum_{\varepsilon=0}^{1} \sum_{i=1}^{\Omega} \tilde{S}_i \Lambda_{ij}\left(\theta_i, \varepsilon\right) match\left(\vartheta, B_{ij}\right) \tag{3.7}$$

35

$$match\,(p,q) = \begin{cases} 1 & p = q \\ 0 & \text{otherwise} \end{cases} \tag{3.8}$$

$$\theta' = \left\langle \frac{N\theta}{2\pi} \right\rangle_N \tag{3.9}$$

where ϑ denotes the angular bin, Ω the local neighborhood of i and $\tilde{S}_i$ the normalized version of the original structure tensor S_i. This is accomplished by scaling the primary eigenvalue to unity while maintaining the original eigenvalue ratio. This reduces the effects of outliers by assigning all points with equal likelihood prior to the diffusion process. Equation 3.9 is used for the discrete case to convert angle θ into the appropriate bin θ'. The $\langle \dots \rangle$ notation denotes a rounding operation and the subscript N denotes periodicity conversion.

In summary, voter i sends a ballot $\tilde{S}_i$, weighted by Λ_{ij}, to bin B_{ij} of receiver j. This stage of processing results in every receiver having a collection of ballots in each of its associated bins. Next, the ballots are averaged *per bin* such that there is a distinct tensor representing each of the N directional bins.

For the first stage of the ATD, the memory requirements are N times higher than anisotropic diffusion and tensor voting, which use a *single* tensor representation, and twice those for relaxation labeling, which uses symmetric information implying only half of the angular range is needed. However, dedicating an angular bin for each *direction*, rather than *orientation*, that allows asymmetric structures, namely junctions, to be revealed.

3.2   Stage Two: Iterative Diffusion of DDF

Once the angular bins of each node have been populated, the local DDF structure is diffused iteratively to its neighbors. This is accomplished through a ROI map and directional bin field that take different forms from those of the first stage. At the beginning of the second stage, the DDF representation has a single structure tensor occupying each of the directional bins. This information must first be transformed from tensor to scalar form creating a one-dimensional DDF (1D-

36

DDF). This is calculated by summing 2π-periodic normalized Gaussians[3], $G_{2\pi}$ as per Equation 3.10:

$$DDF_i\left(\vartheta\right) = \sum_{\beta=1}^{N} |S_\beta|\, G_{2\pi}\left(\theta_\beta, \sigma_{\varsigma_\beta}, \vartheta\right) \qquad (3.10)$$

$$\sigma_\varsigma = (1 - \varsigma)\left(\sigma_{\max} - \sigma_{\min}\right) + \sigma_{\min} \qquad (3.11)$$

where the three Gaussian parameters $(\theta, \sigma, \vartheta)$ correspond to the mean, variance and position respectively. The coherence, ς, is defined as per Equation 2.9. The parameter ϑ ranges between $[0, 2\pi)$ and is subsampled with N increments for the discrete case to correspond with the bounded limits $[-b, b]$. For all of the experiments $b = 3$, which is based on encapsulating 99.7% of the area under the Gaussian when $\sigma = 1$ for $[-b, b]$. The subscript β is used to account for each of the structure tensors stored in the directional bin ϑ. This subscript is not shown in Equation 3.11 for visual clarity. The Gaussian is also amplified by the corresponding structure tensor saliency as defined by Equation 3.3. The values of $(\sigma_{min}, \sigma_{max})$ are chosen empirically as $(0.25, 2)$ to vary between *certain* and *uncertain* estimates as a function of the coherence, which is bounded between $[0, 1]$. The bin-wise tensor responses are transformed into Gaussian functions as Gaussians are able to model the tensor coherence through their variance parameter as well as provide a smooth transition between bins when summed.

The process of transforming the tensor-defined DDF into the scalar or 1D-DDF is illustrated in Figure 3.2. In this example, there are only three bins populated by structure tensors, which are represented in 2D elliptical form in the same manner as Figure 2.11. The first structure tensor in the 40° bin has high coherence as noted by the elongated appearance of the ellipse. This translates into a sharp Gaussian spike centered at 40° in Figure 3.2b. The structure tensor at 230° is also elongated; however, it has a markedly broader shape reflecting less coherence than the first tensor. This creates a Gaussian with greater variance. Since the Gaussians are normalized such that their area under the curve is unity, the second Gaussian is less amplified than the first. Finally, the ball-shaped structure tensor indicates a coherence of zero, meaning that the Gaussian tends toward the largest variance

---

[3]The term *normalized*, in this context, refers to amplifying the Gaussian function such that the total area under the curve sums to one.

allowed, σ_{max}. Summing these Gaussians results in the 1D-DDF and is depicted in Figure 3.2c. When the Gaussians are multiplied by their respective saliency values, the higher certainty measurement at 40° is amplified while the ball-shaped structure tensor at bin 270° is completely eliminated, as illustrated in Figure 3.2d, which better reflects the underlying data.

Next, the 1D-DDF is converted into the ROI map as per Equation 3.12:

$$
\hat{\Lambda}_{ij} = \begin{cases} \frac{1}{N_\Omega} & 0 \le \rho_{ij} < DDF'\left(\varphi_{ij}\right) \\ \frac{1}{N_\Omega} \cos\left[\frac{\pi}{2}\left(\frac{\rho_{ij}-DDF'(\varphi_{ij})}{\rho_{gap}}\right)\right] & DDF'\left(\varphi_{ij}\right) \le \rho_{ij} \le \left[DDF'\left(\varphi_{ij}\right) + \rho_{gap}\right] \\ 0 & \text{otherwise} \end{cases}
$$

$$(3.12)$$

$$
DDF' = \frac{DDF}{DDF_{\max}}\rho_{\min} \tag{3.13}
$$

$$
\rho_{min} + \rho_{gap} = \left(\frac{1}{2}\,scale\right) \tag{3.14}
$$

where ρ_{ij} is the Euclidean distance between nodes i and j, and $\rho_{\min}$ denotes the radial distance after which the drop-off begins, as illustrated in Figure 3.3. The radial length of that decay is denoted as ρ_{gap} and *scale* refers to the dimension of the mask used as the diffusion scale. For the experiments, a heuristic of $\rho_{gap} = \frac{1}{8}$ scale was used that produced satisfactory results during testing. The hat notation denotes the *second stage* of processing. The $\frac{1}{N_\Omega}$ term normalizes $\hat{\Lambda}$ by restricting the maximum possible sum of the elements to equal one where N_Ω is the number of points in the local neighborhood of node i. Equation 3.13 normalizes the values of the *DDF* to a range of $[0, \rho_{min}]$. Examples of this conversion are shown in Figure 3.4.

Once the ROI is calculated, there are two choices relating to *how* the ballots are diffused. The first is the form of the ballot sent from voter to receiver. The second is the choice of node that determines the ballot's influence or *weight*.

3.2.1 Ballot Form

The two ballot forms investigated are the *DDF* and *inward* ballots. The former propagates the entire DDF structure from voter to receiver while the inward ballot

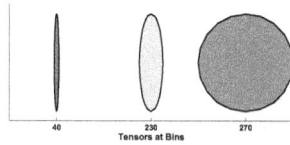

(a)

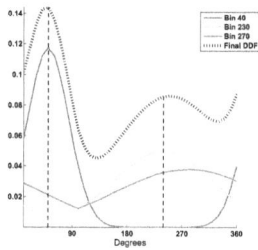

(b)

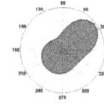

(c)

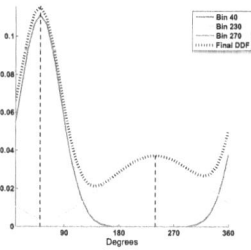

(d)

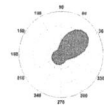

(e)

Figure 3.2: An example of transforming a tensor populated DDF into a 1D-DDF. (a) a DDF with only three tensors at directional bins 40°, 230° and 270°, (b) their corresponding 2π-periodic Gaussians with mean and variance corresponding to the directional bin and coherence in Cartesian form reflected by the black dashed curve and (c) the polar form of (b). (d) the same process but with the Gaussians amplified by their respective gradient saliencies in both Cartesian and (e) the polar form (d).

39

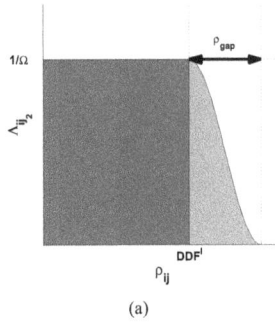

Figure 3.3: Illustration of the radial decay as per Equation 3.12.

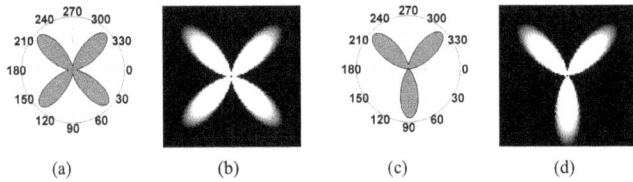

Figure 3.4: (a and c) two 1D-DDFs in polar form and (b and d) their corresponding spatial-based region-of-influence (ROI) function, $\hat{\Lambda}_{ij}$ respectively.

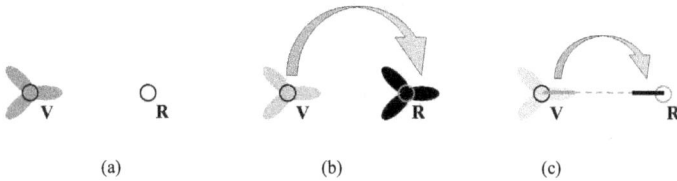

Figure 3.5: Ballot Types: (a) given a 'Y' shaped DDF at the voter 'V', (b) propagate to receiver 'R' using the DDF ballot or (c) the inward ballot approach where the dashed line denotes the common ray between the voter and the receiver.

sends a single value taken from the angular bin of the voter that is directed towards the receiver. This distinction is made as the DDF ballot type is the method most used in previous methods while the inward ballot has the added benefit of being derived from a co-nodal property[4]. This is collected into the angular bin at the receiver that is directed back towards the voter. These ballot types are illustrated in Figure 3.5, which depicts a 'Y'-shaped DDF at voter 'V' that is to be propagated to the receiver 'R'.

For the inward ballot approach, an additional step is performed when the angular bin chosen is not populated by a tensor, as in the sparsely populated DDF in the example of Figure 3.2a. In this case, the structure tensors from the populated bins are spread into empty bins using element-wise linear interpolation of the structure tensors. This process is illustrated in Figure 3.6 where a DDF initially with only three populated bins (1,5, and 9) are interpolated into bins 2-4 and 6-8. The additional step addresses the problems resulting from discretization. Without it, there would be no information propagated from bin 2, even though there is a strong response in the neighborhing bin 1.

3.2.2   Node Choice for ROI

Another consideration for this second stage is to define the ROI map using either the voter or receiver node. These approaches are compared using the DDF ballot

---

[4]Co-nodal refers to the property of being dependent on both the voter and the receiver's spatial location and properties

41

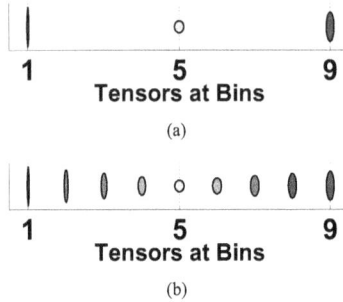

1   5   9
Tensors at Bins

(a)

1   5   9
Tensors at Bins

(b)

Figure 3.6: (a) Initial DDF with only three tensors (at bins 1, 5 and 9) populated by empty bins between them, (b) results of interpolating tensor-wise for stage two.

in Figure 3.7. The initial DDF for voter 'V' indicates strong estimates along the horizontal orientation by the lobes aligned along 0° and 180° while the receiver has vertical estimates along 90° and 270°, as illustrated in Figure 3.7a. For the voter-centered (VC) approach, Figure 3.7b, the weighting of the ballot propagated from the voter to the receiver is a function of the DDF centered at the *voter*. The ROI centered at 'V' dictates the weight of the ballot in this example. Since proximity is also a parameter in the creation of the DDF-shaped ROI, the ballot sent has less influence hence is smaller than the original. This approach is the typical approach for most diffusion techniques where ballots are based solely on the data at the voter's location. In contrast, for the receiver-centered (RC) approach illustrated in Figure 3.7c, the weighting map is derived from the DDF centered at the *receiver*. Only those voters located within the ROI are taken into account. Since, in this example, the original DDF at the receiver is oriented vertically, and the voter is not encompassed within the receiver's ROI, only the original DDF from 'R' is used to create the DDF for the next iteration.

The following sections examine the various combinations of ballot types and ROIs in further detail.

3.2.3   Voter-Centered, DDF Ballot

The first method considered is to diffuse DDF ballots weighted by the ROI as a function of the voter. This approach is called the *voter-centered, DDF ballot* (VC-DDF) [3]. This setup has a similar approach to standard diffusion methods where

42

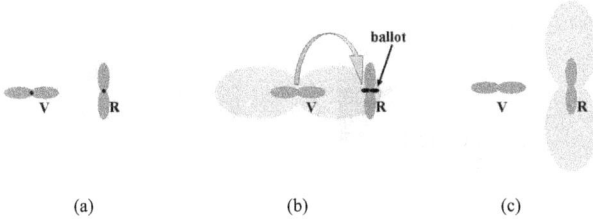

| (a) | (b) | (c) |

Figure 3.7: (a) Original input: two nodes where voter 'V' exhibits a horizontal hypothesis while receiver 'R' has a vertical hypothesis, (b) illustrating how ballots are collected at 'R' for the voter-centered and (c) the receiver-centered approach. The light gray, dark gray and black denote the ROI, initial DDFs and the ballot sent from the voter to the receiver respectively.

a central estimate, DDF in this case, is propagated from the voter to the receiver, weighted by an influence function. The voting field for this approach is defined as:

$$\hat{\Gamma}_{ij}(\vartheta) = \hat{\Lambda}_{ij} DDF_i(\vartheta) \tag{3.15}$$

where $\hat{\Gamma}_{ij}$ reflects the *ballot field* that voter i sends to receiver j and Λ_{ij} is defined as per Equation 3.6. The ballots are collected at receiver j by summing bin-wise (per ϑ).

$$\hat{\Upsilon}_j(\vartheta) = \sum_{i=1,\ i\neq j}^{\Omega} \hat{\Gamma}_{ij}(\vartheta) \tag{3.16}$$

where the $\hat{\Upsilon}$ denotes the DDF results of the diffusion, Ω is the neighborhood of j and $i \neq j$ is to prevent the ballot information at node j from being used twice in the iterative framework that follows. This new collection of ballots is offset by the original DDF at the receiver through the following iterative update:

$$DDF_j^t(\vartheta) = \alpha DDF_j^{t-1}(\vartheta) + (1-\alpha) DDF_j^{D,t-1}(\vartheta) \tag{3.17}$$

43

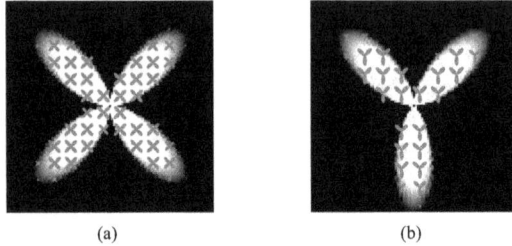

(a)   (b)

Figure 3.8: (a and b) the ballot fields associated with the $\hat{\Lambda}_{ij}$ weighting maps from Figure 3.4 for an X-shaped DDF and a Y-shaped DDF at the voter respectively. The background image depicts the ROI while the individual overlaid 'X' and 'Y' shapes represent the ballots.

where α denotes the diffusion or learning coefficient that is bounded between $[0, 1]$ and t represents the iteration time step. The diffusion coefficient constrains the degree of updating of data that takes place at each iteration. Two example ballot fields are illustrated in Figure 3.8 associated with the respective 'X' and 'Y' shaped $\hat{\Lambda}_{ij}$ maps of Figure 3.4. The original shape of the DDF at the voter determines *both* the ROI weighting map *and* the ballots themselves in this setup.

3.2.4 Receiver-Centered, DDF Ballot

The receiver-centered approach uses the DDF representation at the *receiver*, rather than the voter, to weight the incoming ballots. This requires special attention to be paid to the ordering of the subscripts of the $\hat{\Lambda}$ function. In general, $\hat{\Lambda}_{ab}$ is read as the weighting based on the DDF at node a projected to node b. Thus, for a receiver-centered ROI, receiver j collects a ballot from voter i weighted with respect to j. The DDF results of the diffusion D are defined as per Equations (3.18-3.19):

$$\hat{\Gamma}_{ji}(\vartheta) = \hat{\Lambda}_{ji} DDF_i(\vartheta) \tag{3.18}$$

$$\hat{\Upsilon}_j(\vartheta) = \sum_{i=1,\ i\neq j}^{\Omega} \hat{\Gamma}_{ji}(\vartheta) \tag{3.19}$$

44

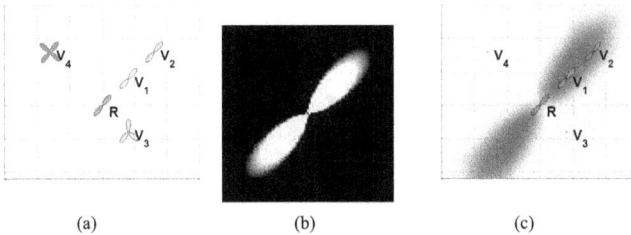

Figure 3.9: (a) A test case for the receiver-centered DDF ballot approach. A receiving node 'R' (center) and four neighboring voting nodes ($V_1 - V_4$), (b) the associated $\hat{\Lambda}_{ji}$ corresponding to the receiver, (c) $\hat{\Lambda}_{ji}$ overlaid in the spatial domain where the color intensity corresponds to the strength of the weight.

This $\hat{\Upsilon}$ is then used in the iterative update Equation 3.17. An example of this approach is shown in Figure 3.9. The DDF is represented in polar form where the center node is labeled as the receiver and the remaining four nodes as voters. The $\hat{\Lambda}_{ji}$ is calculated with respect to the DDF of the receiver and is depicted in Figure 3.9b, which is used to weight the ballot field $\hat{\Gamma}_{ji}$. This approach favors the receiving DDF characteristics and handles noisy or outlier DDF structures as it is updated by the more common structures that fall within the scope of the associated $\hat{\Lambda}_{ji}$ because of the co-nodal characteristic previously discussed. This characteristic is examined further in the next chapter.

3.2.5 Voter-Centered, Inward Ballot

Although the DDF ballot type seems appropriate for most applications, its ability to represent multiple estimates is also its weakness. This is due to the fact that in the diffusion step, propagating the entire DDF results in too many directional estimates at each node.

For example, in Figure 3.10a, the four DDFs can be connected to indicate two lines meeting at a corner, P_3, through the percepts of continuity and proximity. Nodes P_1 and P_4 would be end-points of the two lines while P_2 would become a segment of a line, denoted as a horizontal structure. Using DDF ballots, however, gives rise to four directional estimates at P_3. In other words, the resulting DDF

45

(a)   (b)

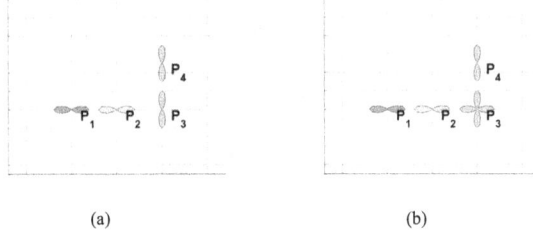

Figure 3.10: Test case where propagating π-periodic DDFs with the voter-centered DDF ballot approach produces symmetric artifacts at the junction. (a) initial set of DDFs at four nodes and (b) results after one iteration of ATD (VC-DDF).

may become π-periodic even when the ROI function is asymmetric. As the case against symmetric structures has already been addressed, the focus here will be on designing a method by which asymmetric structures are created or maintained. The solution is to propagate only a select portion of the DDF from node to node. One such approach investigated is the *voter-centered, inward ballot* (VC-IB) [4], in which the directional bin field is calculated as:

$$\hat{B}_{ij} = \varphi_{ij} + \pi \tag{3.20}$$

and the update equation:

$$\hat{\Upsilon}_j\left(\vartheta\right) = \sum_{i=1,\; i\neq j}^{\Omega} \hat{\Lambda}_{ij} DDF_i\left(\varphi_{ij}\right) match\left(\vartheta, \hat{B}_{ij}\right) \tag{3.21}$$

where the *match* function is defined in Equation 3.8. Examples of these inward-facing ballot fields are illustrated in Figure 3.11.

3.2.6   Receiver-Centered, Inward Ballot

The last approach to investigate uses the inward ballot form with the ROI as a function of the receiver. The directional bin field is calculated as per Equation 3.22 (note the ordering of the indices):

46

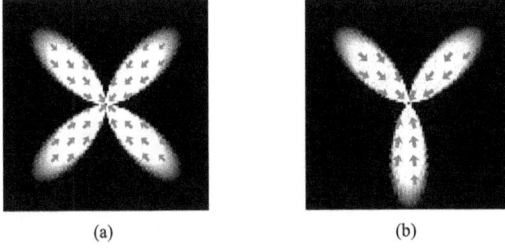

(a)   (b)

Figure 3.11: (a and b) using $\hat{\Lambda}_{ij}$ for both an 'X' and 'Y'-shaped DDFs of Figure 3.4, the inward ballot field is overlaid where the vector directions determines the direction-based bin that is updated at that node and the magnitudes indicate the weighting.

$$\hat{B}_{ji} = \varphi_{ji} + \pi \tag{3.22}$$

Thus values are *taken* from voters and *collected* at the receiver. The corresponding directional bin at the receiver is calculated along the direction from receiver j to voter i as:

$$\hat{\Upsilon}_j(\vartheta) = \sum_{i=1,\ i\neq j}^{\Omega} \hat{\Lambda}_{ji} DDF_i\left(\hat{B}_{ji}\right) match\left(\vartheta, \varphi_{ji}\right) \tag{3.23}$$

where φ_{ji} is the direction from receiver j to voter i with respect to the x-axis. The general process for this approach is illustrated in Figure 3.12. The inward ballots of the voters with respect to the receiver are then determined. Note that only V_1 and V_3 have strong ballots whereas V_2 sends no ballot as its receiver-directed bin is zero. This behavior enforces local support as V_1 and V_3 are connected through the receiver in an obtuse-angled corner structure, whereas V_2 is perpendicular to the lobe pointing toward it from the receiver. Once the ballots are weighted by the ROI function, they are collected at the receiver to form $\hat{\Upsilon}_j$ and are incorporated using iteration Equation 3.17 to form the new DDF as displayed in Figure 3.12d.

47

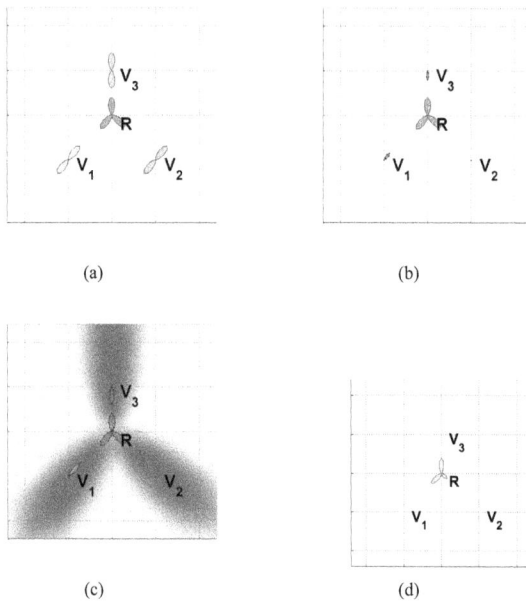

Figure 3.12: A test case for the receiver-centered, inward ballot approach. (a) initial DDFs per node where the receiver 'R' is the center node surrounded by three voters, (b) the inward bin of each voter's DDF value is isolated, (c) then weighted according to $\hat{\Lambda}_{ji}$ and (d) the resulting DDF at the receiver.

3.3   Design Considerations

Several percepts were considered in the design of the ATD. For example, *proximity* is introduced by incorporating radial decay into the creation of the ROI. Also, *closure* is addressed if the diffusion performs *dense voting*, where empty nodes are populated by the iterative diffusion from non-empty nodes. *Similarity* is enforced by choosing the DDF ballot, as this approach strengthens nodes with similar DDFs. In contrast, *curvilinearity* and *continuity* are promoted by the inward ballot. These phenomena are explored further in Chapter 5.

The proposed ATD method has several characteristics in common with the generalized relaxation labeling (RL) approach. For example, where RL updates the estimates of labels among nodes, ATD updates estimates at each direction θ among nodes. Also, the probability of label λ at node i for RL is similar to the parameter of a single angular bin θ with the DDF structure. There are also some key differences between these approaches. The compatibility function $r_{ij}(\lambda, \lambda')$ can be thought of as a weighting map similar to the $\hat{\Lambda}_{ij}$ in the ATD approach. Whereas r_{ij} is symmetric, $r_{ij}(\lambda, \lambda') = r_{ji}(\lambda', \lambda)$, the same is not true of its equivalent $\hat{\Lambda}_{ij}$ in the ATD approach. In the latter, the weighting sent from node i to node j depends on the DDF representation centered at node i, which is potentially different from j. Furthermore, ATD uses the entire DDF information at a given node in the creation of the weighting map, whereas the RL approach uses a weight based solely on the information from a pair of angular bins between nodes. Most importantly, ATD incorporates an orientation-to-direction transformation in its first stage of processing that allows for the asymmetric representation of structure.

It should be noted that ATD is not scale invariant, as there is a diffusion scale parameter in this method. However, this approach does, to a certain extent, address the issue of scale through two methods. First, the approach is iterative with a spatially defined neighborhood. This implies that local structural estimates are diffused to approximate the estimates that have the greatest support regardless of scale. Second, the ROI has a proximity-defined drop-off that is proportional to the DDF at each of the nodes. This means that strong estimates have influence over a larger scale than those with weak estimates.

49

Chapter 4

Design Analysis

There are four different approaches associated with ATD: the voter-centered DDF ballot (VC-DDF), voter-centered inward ballot (VC-IB), receiver-centered DDF ballot (RC-DDF) and the receiver-centered inward ballot (RC-IB). Within each of these approaches, there are several different options from which to choose. The following sections detail the relative merits of each design module and their effects on asymmetric structure representations. First, the difference between the DDF and inward ballots is explored followed by a comparison of the voter- and receiver-centered voting methodologies. Next, the utility of structural biasing using the DDF-shaped ROI rather than an isotropic function is examined. Other considerations such as the choice between sparse and dense voting, inward versus parallel voting fields and tests for convergence are also addressed.

4.1 DDF versus Inward Ballots

The approach of propagating a directionally based ballot, rather than the entire DDF representation, is key to the identification of asymmetric information. The effects of such an approach are best illustrated with an example. Consider the node-wise DDF configurations of Figure 4.1. At each of the four nodes, a two-lobed DDF is initialized. Three of the four indicate an initial vertical estimate while the fourth indicates horizontal orientation. The respective ROI maps determine either the weighting map to propagate the voter's ballot to the receivers (VC) or the collection of voters whose ballots are biased with respect to the receiver (RC).

50

(a)

(b)   (c)   (d)   (e)

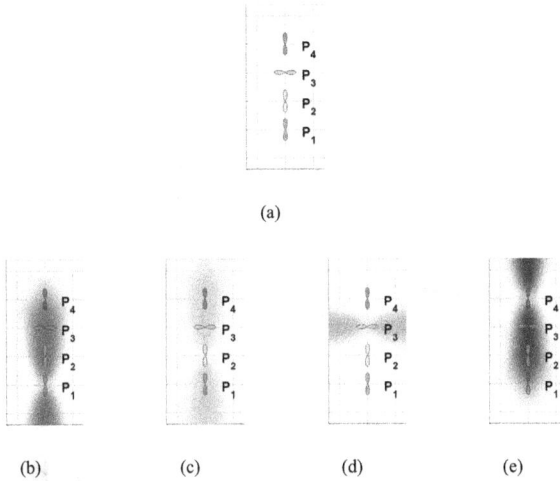

Figure 4.1: (a) original DDF configuration from stage one of ATD, (b-e) overlaid ROI associated with each of the nodes $(P_1 - P_4)$ respectively.

First, the difference between the DDF and inward ballots (IB) is examined in the VC and RC contexts. For the following test cases, sparse, as opposed to dense voting, is applied.

In Table 4.1, the VC-DDF approach is applied. The top row illustrates the raw DDF ballots while those in the second row are weighted with respect to the ROI map. For this layout, the node with the horizontal orientation is assigned the label P_3. In the second row of P_3 there are no horizontal ballots propagated to the other three nodes, hence reducing the contribution of this outlier within the first iteration. Meanwhile, the consensus of the remaining nodes dictates a vertically oriented line as shown in the third row of Table 4.1, by the creation of two vertically oriented lobes at P_3. For each successive iteration, the initial horizontal estimate of P_3 is reduced while the vertical estimate, which reflects the majority, is strengthened.

The same observations can be made for the VC-IB approach in that the influence of P_3 is reduced; however, the overall estimates are quite different. As shown in the first row of Table 4.2, the ballots are formed from a single angular bin of

51

Table 4.1: Voter-Centered, DDF Ballots: (First row) the ballots sent from node P to its neighbors with the ROI overlaid, where the size of the DDFs denotes saliency, (second row) the ballots now weighted by the ROI, and (third row) results of collecting the ballots node-wise after one and four iterations respectively.

the original DDF at each node. Note in particular that the DDF at P_3 propagates no ballots to its neighbors. This layout also highlights the formation of end-point junctions, such as at P_1 and P_4 where there is co-nodal support along a single direction. This results from the gradual transformation of the initial two-lobed DDFs to a single lobe representation that now indicates endpoints of a common vertical line, as shown in the third row of Table 4.2.

By propagating only the inward ballot in the VC approach, asymmetric structural features (end-points in the above example) can be created from initially *symmetric* DDFs. Although the propagation of DDF ballots reduced the P_3 outlier, this is not capable of *creating* an asymmetric DDF.

Next, the effects of propagating DDF versus inward ballots are examined within the receiver-centered (RC) approach. In Table 4.3, DDF ballots are propagated from the voters to the four receivers. The first row depicts the unweighted, DDF ballots while the second row weights them according to the receiver's ROI map. For this approach, the effects of the outlier at P_3 are far more apparent. The neighboring nodes incorporate this DDF in its entirety resulting in a ringing of the horizontal data from P_3 throughout the nodes. After the first iteration as shown in the third row, the relative saliency of P_3 itself is reduced, as noted by the smaller DDF at P_3, however, there are now horizontal estimates in all of the neighboring nodes as well. After four iterations P_3 is eliminated, as is expected of an outlier; however, P_4, which clearly supports the vertical estimate initially, has also been significantly reduced in saliency. Both P_1 and P_2 have retained the mutually supported vertical estimates, but now include a lesser horizontal estimate as well. Clearly, using the RC-DDF approach is not a desirable approach for representing the underlying asymmetric structure.

Using the inward ballot approach addresses the issues associated with the DDF ballot, as shown in Table 4.4. Using this ballot type, the disagreement between the horizontal estimate at P_3 and those of its neighbors is resolved. Note that the information at the top-most node, P_4, remains salient after four iterations by depicting an end-point.

The inward ballot scheme is superior to the DDF ballot approach for both the VC and RC approaches in that it properly retains co-nodal structural estimates that agree, while weakening those that do not, as per the diffusion philosophy. Also, it allows for the transformation of symmetric to asymmetric DDFs that provide a more accurate representation of the underlying structure.

	P_1	P_2	P_3	P_4
Original Ballots	P4 P3 P2 P1	P4 P3 P2 P1	P4 P3 P2 P1	P4 P3 P2 P1
ROI-weighted Ballots	P4 P3 P2 P1	P4 P3 P2 P1	P4 P3 P2 P1	P4 P3 P2 P1

	One Iteration	Four Iterations
	P4 P3 P2 P1	P4 P3 P2 P1

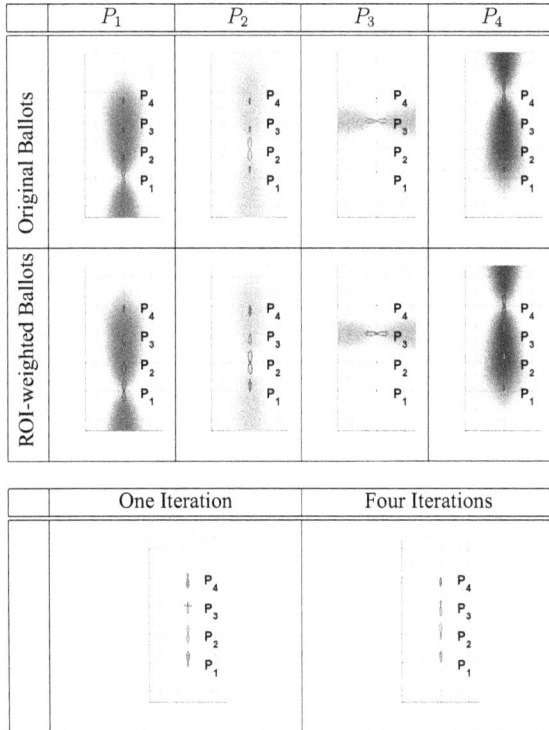

Table 4.2: Voter-Centered, Inward Ballots: (First row) the *inward* ballots sent from node P to its neighbors with the ROI overlaid, where the size of the DDFs denotes saliency. Note that the ballots have been widened for visual purposes only resulting in drop-shaped lobes, (second row) the ballots now weighted by the ROI, and (third row) results of collecting the ballots node-wise after one and four iterations respectively.

	P_1	P_2	P_3	P_4
Original Ballots	V_3 V_2 V_1 R	V_3 V_2 R V_1	V_3 R V_2 V_1	R V_3 V_2 V_1
ROI-weighted Ballots	V_3 V_2 V_1 R	V_3 V_2 R V_1	V_3 R V_2 V_1	R V_3 V_2 V_1

	One Iteration	Four Iterations
	P_4 P_3 P_2 P_1	P_4 P_3 P_2 P_1

Table 4.3: Receiver-Centered, DDF Ballots: (First row) the ballots sent from voters $(V_1 - V_3)$ to receiver R, (second row) the ballots now weighted by the ROI centered at R, and (third row) results of collecting the ballots node-wise after one and four iterations respectively.

	P_1	P_2	P_3	P_4
Original Ballots	V_3 V_2 V_1 R	V_3 V_2 R V_1	V_3 R V_2 V_1	R V_3 V_2 V_1
ROI-weighted Ballots	V_3 V_2 V_1 R	V_3 V_2 R V_1	V_3 R V_2 V_1	R V_3 V_2 V_1

	One Iteration	Four Iterations
	P_4 P_3 P_2 P_1	P_4 P_3 P_2 P_1

Table 4.4: Receiver-Centered, Inward Ballots: (First row) the *inward* ballots sent from voters $(V_1 - V_3)$ to receiver R, (second row) the ballots now weighted by the ROI centered at R, and (third row) results of collecting the ballots node-wise after one and four iterations respectively.

Table 4.5: (first row) original node layout, (second row) VC-IB after one and four iterations respectively, and (third row) RC-IB for one and four iterations respectively.

4.2 Voter- versus Receiver-Centered

Both the voter- and receiver-centered approaches offer distinct advantages for the diffusion of asymmetric DDFs. As the previous section has already demonstrated the advantage of the inward ballot over the DDF ballot, we now focus on a comparison of the VC-IB and RC-IB.

For the DDF configuration in Table 4.5, three of the four nodes have vertical orientations while a fourth has a horizontal estimate. Note that these are the same DDFs as those in Figure 4.1, but with a different spatial layout.

Using either the VC-IB or RC-IB approach, the structural co-nodal agreement between P_1 and P_3 is strengthened, as noted by the persistent appearance of lobes that point towards one another after four iterations. Furthermore, the lobe at P_1

that initially points downwards is iteratively weakened as there is no corresponding node below to support this hypothesis.

The most striking difference between the two approaches is how the DDF at P_2 is handled. For the VC-IB, the left-pointing lobe of P_2 is propagated to P_1 where both P_1 and P_2 iterate towards a corner or 'L'-type junction. Furthermore, there is greater saliency or certainty[1] that a corner junction is located at P_1 than at P_2 as noted by the larger DDF. This occurs as there is greater support for the consensus of such a structure between P_1 and P_3, which initially point directly at one another. This contrasts with the relationship between P_3 and P_4 that are mutually parallel in the original layout. Conversely, the RC-IB approach uses the DDF at P_2 to dictate which voters to take into account. Although only P_1 is initially included, the value of the inward ballot at P_1 that points towards P_2 is zero. This implies that the relative saliency of P_2 is weaker compared to P_1 and P_3 where co-nodal agreement is being strengthened. This difference highlights how VC-IB and RC-IB address outlier nodes that do not agree with the majority of the neighbors. In this case, the VC-IB tends to adapt the outlier at P_2 into the most likely structure with respect to the other nodes by forming a corner junction while the RC-IB tends to reduce its saliency.

Another difference between the two approaches is how the DDF at P_4 is handled. In the VC-IB approach, ballots are sent from P_4 to P_2 based solely on data from P_4. This has the effect of strengthening estimates *between* populated nodes. Since P_4 is directed towards P_2, the lobes between them are strengthened. The end effect is that the initially two-lobed DDF of P_4 tends to shift towards a contour estimate *between* P_4 and P_2 in that these points now become potential *end-points* for a common line. This is illustrated in the second column of VC-IB in Table 4.5 where P_4 tends towards a single lobe pointing downward, which indicates an end-point. In the RC-IB approach, however, the focus remains on strengthening existing co-nodal structural estimates, i.e. reinforcing lobes that point between one another. Since the only voter that falls within the ROI of P_4 is P_2, and the inward-ballot from P_2 is zero, the saliency of the DDF at P_4 is gradually weakened.

These observations can be generalized as follows:

O_1. *VC-IB tends to adapt outlier nodes into a structural representation that*

---

[1]A DDF expresses a directional estimate through its local maxima. The saliency or certainty of the estimate is calculated by finding the area of the lobe associated with the estimate.

agrees with the rest of its neighbors

O_2. *RC-IB reduces the saliency of outlier nodes, similar to noise reduction, while strengthening estimates between nodes that agree on the local structure*

These are supported by the results in Tables (4.2 and 4.4). The VC-IB approach has replaced the outlier from P_3 with a vertically oriented DDF, (Table 4.2, third row) strengthening the estimate held by the majority of the nodes, while the RC-IB reduces P_3 with respect to the neighboring nodes (Table 4.4, third row).

A third and final node layout is examined in Table 4.6, where the outlier, P_4 in this case, is no longer spatially aligned with the predominant, vertical structural estimate of nodes P_1 through P_3. Again, the RC-IB approach reduces the saliency of the outlier. This time, however, the VC-IB approach does not replaced P_4 to conform to the predominant estimate, but rather reduces its saliency. This, nevertheless, is in accordance with the earlier observations. The predominant underlying structure is a vertical line from P_1 to P_3. There is little structural agreement between P_1 and P_4, i.e. there are no inwardly facing lobes between these two nodes. Thus P_4 should not become a part of this pattern. The same is true between P_2 and P_4. Therefore, the structural representation detailed in O_1 refers to both how the individual node is shaped by its DDF as well as how it relates to the estimated structure of local neighborhood.

4.3   Role of DDF-Shaped ROI

To investigate the importance of the DDF-shaped ROI, the results for the RC approach were calculated using both an isotropic 2D Gaussian function and the DDF-shaped ROI as defined in Equation 3.12. This comparison was first investigated using structure tensor layouts in both 'T' and 'X'-type configurations [3]. In this work, a corner-type structure tensor layout is used, as in Table 4.7, to highlight the differences between these ROI maps.

Within the RC approach, the ROI weights the ballots of the voters that are collected at the receiver. For an isotropic ROI, ballots are accepted from all voters and weighted solely based on relative proximity. The result of this voting approach is a blurring effect within the DDFs at each of the nodes, as shown in the first column of Table 4.7. These results could be interpreted to highlight the node with the

59

Table 4.6: (first row) original node layout, (second row) VC-IB after one and four iterations respectively, and (third row) RC-IB for one and four iterations respectively.

largest saliency as the location of the corner junction; however, much information is lost in this process. For example, the location of the original edges as well as their respective orientations are not preserved in the final result. Another drawback of the isotropic ROI is that nodes with non-zero DDFs have equal influence as empty nodes. The data is diffused to the empty nodes in a dense voting manner, without the benefit of structural information. This effect is eliminated when the isotropic ROI is replaced by the DDF-shaped ROI as shown in the second column of Table 4.7c. The originally empty nodes now weight all incoming ballots to zero. This implies that the DDF-shaped ROI restricts the maximum number of non-zero nodes only to those that had non-zero DDFs in the original information. Finally, the resulting DDFs are able to enforce structural estimates of local support by strengthening relationships between nodes of similar DDF shapes.

The same general effects can be observed using the RC-IB approach. With the isotropic ROI, data is propagated to the initially empty nodes, as shown in the first column of Table 4.7. With the DDF-shaped ROI, the original locations of the DDFs are indicated clearly by non-empty nodes while specific DDFs denote end-points, as shown in the second column of Table 4.7.

4.4   Sparse versus Dense Voting

Sparse voting implies that votes are only propagated to non-empty nodes such that the number of initialized nodes at $t = 0$ remains fixed throughout the experiment. In contrast, *dense voting* populates all of the empty nodes, which is typically performed to add structure to sparse data.

Since sparse voting uses only a subset of the total nodes, it requires less memory and processing time. The advantage of dense voting is that it is able to fill in missing gaps between similar structures. This mimics the percept of *closure* by populating empty nodes with the local structural estimate. This effect is demonstrated in Figure 4.2 where empty nodes between the original two estimates are populated and form a single contour estimate.

Table 4.7: (first row) corner-shaped DDF layout, (second row) results using RC-DDF approach with the isotropic ROI and DDF-shaped ROI respectively and (third row) results using the RC-IB approach with the isotropic ROI and the DDF-shaped ROI respectively.

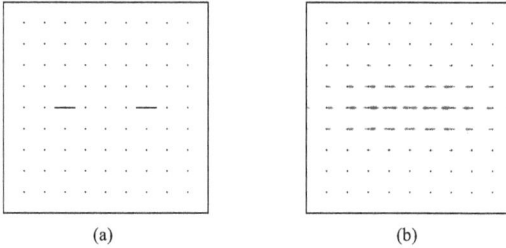

Figure 4.2: (a) two horizontal tensors separated by a gap and (b) the effects of dense voting with the VC-IB approach, which populates the area between the gap.

4.5   Inward versus Parallel Ballots

In the first stage of the ATD approach, ballots are directed *parallel* to the original tensor rather than *inward* towards the center. Although the primary motivation was to reduce initial biasing of the data, this also simplifies the estimates of the underlying structure. For example, given a 'T'-shaped tensor layout as shown in Figure 4.3a, the inward and parallel choices each produce markedly different results. For example, if the ballots are chosen to face inward toward the center of the original data, the underlying 'T'-junction is represented properly; however, two curves are also depicted between the points (P1,P2) and (P1,P3). The much simpler representation of the 'T'-junction is created when initializing stage one of the ATD with parallel ballots as shown in Figure 4.3c. This philosophy is motivated by that of Occam's Razor where the simplest representation proves the most fruitful [2]. This choice is less clear if there are only two initial tensors in a configuration as (P1,P2) alone from Figure 4.3a. Whether it is better to choose a rounded curve or a sharp corner between the two estimates will normally be application dependent.

4.6   Different Data Domains

The ATD approach can be applied to a variety of input types as long as there is a way to transform this data into a tensor field. One example is a *point-cloud* that comprises a collection of discrete points in space. This data can be seeded

63

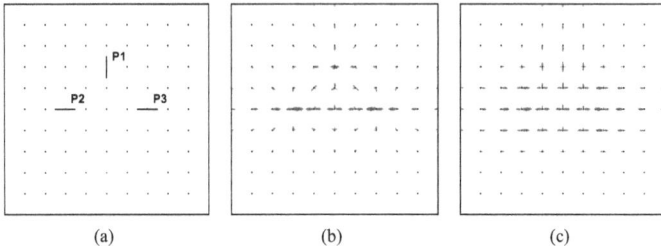

Figure 4.3: (a) tensor layout with three tensors forming a 'T' junction separated by a gap and (b and c) the effects of using inward directed and parallel ballots for stage one respectively. The VC-IB approach were used for both results.

with directional estimates by applying the ball voting field of the tensor voting approach [52], which creates a tensor field. Another input type is a scalar field, such as a 2D image. This data can be transformed into a tensor field by constructing a gradient-based structure tensor at each location. Finally a vector field can be used directly in the ATD approach by converting each vector into a stick-tensor or by implementing a vector-field version of the proposed approach.

The ability of the ATD to function on a wide variety of input types is a clear advantage over convolution methods that were designed only for the scalar domain.

4.7 Encoding Curvature Information

By storing the local structural information in DDF form, it is possible to estimate the curvature value without explicitly identifying the local correspondence between nodes. With a single structure tensor representation, one possible method that avoids testing a large set of node pairs is to convert the tensors into the (X, θ)-space where θ is the direction of $\vec{e}_1$ and $X = (x, y)$. The Hough transform could then be applied to identify points along common lines. This particular approach has several disadvantages including the standard bin-size problem associated with the Hough transform[2], the need for a methodology to identify points along a curve rather than a line, and is computationally expensive [25]. The advantage of the dif-

---

[2]The scale of the region in which the points are collected greatly affects the results.

64

fusion approach is in its enforcement of local support that encodes the structural correspondence between nodes indirectly, thus avoiding the need to address this issue explicitly.

However, this encoding cannot discern between a corner junction and a point indicative of a curve. Resolving this challenge would most likely require the correspondence issue to be addressed after all and as such is left as future work.

4.8 Complexity

To compare the complexity between the diffusion approaches, first assume that the voting fields for both the tensor voting and stage one of the ATD are calculated a priori. Let n represent the number of pixels in the local neighborhood and m is the number of angular bins, the tensor voting method has complexity at $O(n)$. Next, the relaxation labeling approach is $O(\frac{1}{2}nm)$ as it only uses half of the available bins due to its symmetric nature. The complexity of stage one of the ATD method is $O(nm)$, while the secondary stage requires $O(4mn)$ as several additional calculations such as the transformation from the tensor-based DDF to the 1D-DDF as well as the conversion into the region of interest map must be calculated at each pixel. Clearly, the ATD approach is the most computationally intensive of these methods. However, this cost can be justified by the improved results that are obtained, as described in the following chapter.

4.9 Convergence Tests

It is important that the results of the ATD algorithm converge over time to a stable value. Through the normalization of the DDF information as well as that of the ROI map, the DDFs are bounded, as shown in Appendix A. Also, given that a DDF tends toward an estimate that is shared by the majority of its neighbors, only strong underlying structures will produce DDFs with strong estimates. Otherwise, the DDFs will tend toward zero, which implies that their respective ROIs will also restrict their influence. In other words, all DDFs either approach zero or maximum saliency. Convergence can be enforced in the application version of the ATD by defining the learning coefficient as a decreasing function with the iteration count as its parameter. However, in practice, such a function is not necessary as the per iteration changes in DDF values decrease monotonically over time. Usually no more than four iterations are required to reach a change in DDF value less than 25% of that achieved between the first and second iteration. The theoretical foundation for the convergence of the ATD is left as future work.

Chapter 5

Experimental Evaluation

The merits of the ATD approach were evaluated through comparison with the convolution and diffusion approaches. The first test was to assess its accuracy in identifying the gradient directions of a T-junction input image against *convolution* approaches. Next, ATD was compared against *diffusion* techniques in the tensor field domain to highlight the advantage of an asymmetric DDF representation. For all of the tests, the number of angular increments was set to $N = 36$ (10° per bin).

5.1   Convolution Methods

Several different trials were performed in comparing ATD against convolution approaches. The first was to assess the accuracy in identifying a single T-junction pattern with multiple spatial frequencies. The second trial was designed to measure the error for a set of T-junction patterns over a range of single spatial frequencies. The last trial was to assess the error when increasing amounts of additive Gaussian noise was applied.

5.1.1   Off-Center T-Junction Trial

For the first trial, a test-image was designed with *off-center* gradient information,[1] as shown in Figure 5.1a. The results of the convolution approaches are shown in Figure 2.5. All methods used a scale of 11x11 pixels, to match the size of the test image, and the parameters were assigned as follows: Gabor and one-sided

---

[1]Off-center refers to edges that do not radiate from the center of the image. In other words, gradient contours that do not intersect with the center of the swatch.

(a)   (b)

Figure 5.1: (a) input image (reprinted from Figure 2.5a) and (b) the DDF for ATD VC-IB.

$\sigma_x = \sigma_y = 1$, $f = \frac{1}{3}$, the wedge-filter and RAWM used $\frac{\pi}{3}$ for their angular wedge size.

The Gabor and Fourier approaches both identified the horizontal orientation, where the Fourier represented the vertical orientation with more certainty than the Gabor; however, due to the symmetric design of these methods, they were unable to represent the *absence* of vertical edges in the bottom half of the image. The one-sided, wedge and the RAWM methods did not adapt well to the presence of off-center edges. In contrast, the ATD using a VC-IB approach, which performed two iterations of its second stage, depicted estimates aligned properly with the gradient directions from the test case as shown in Figure 5.1b.

5.1.2   Error Measurement

In orientation analysis, both the angular deviation as well as the difference in saliency values between the estimates and ground truths need to be addressed in the calculation of error. Consider the ground truth DDF in Figure 5.2a. If only the angular deviation were used as an error measure, the first test case would have an error of zero, as illustrated in Figure 5.2e, as all directions are aligned with those of the ground truth. Clearly, these two DDFs are different, therefore an error of zero is not appropriate. Using only the difference in saliencies between pairs of ground truth and estimate lobes, as in Figure 5.2f, the error again is zero. This results from the estimate directed northwest being closest, in angular terms, to the ground truth pointing west, both of which have equal saliencies in this case. Again, an error of zero masks the fact that the DDFs are actually different. Another approach is to calculate the SSD between the ground truth and estimates per angular bin to represent the error. Visually, this would correspond to the non-

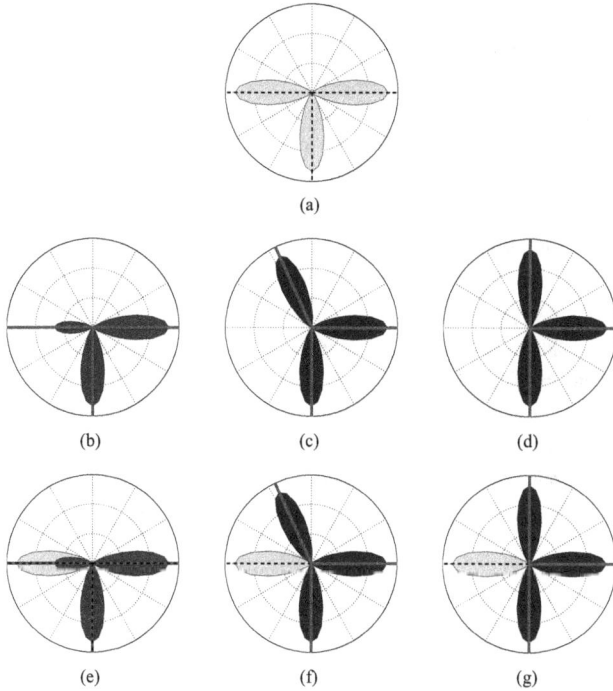

Figure 5.2: (a) DDF for the ground-truth model of a T-junction, and (b-d) three sample DDFs. Using only angular deviation produces zero error for the first sample, which is shown overlaid in (e). Using only the saliency difference between nearest ground-truth and the estimates, where saliency is represented as lobe sizes, is also insufficient as shown in (f) where there clearly exists an error between these DDFs. The SSD results in no difference in error between sample (c) and (d) where (d) overlaps the ground truth in (g). The dashed and solid radial lines aligned with the lobes depict the angular estimates for the ground truth and measured DDFs respectively.

overlapping area between the two DDFs. Although computationally efficient, the angular-based pairing between closest lobes is lost in this process. This implies that equal errors would result from both test cases in Figures 5.2(c and d) where their respective lobes that are directed upward both exhibit no overlap with the ground truth's westward estimate. Clearly, the test case from Figure 5.2c is closer to the model than the DDF in Figure 5.2d and should exhibit a reduced error value.

To account properly for both the angular deviation and the saliency differences, the following error calculation was constructed. First, ground truths and estimates were paired by first associating each estimate with the closest (angular) ground truth. This implies that each ground truth may have zero, one or multiple estimates associated with it. For ground truths with multiple estimates, only the closest estimate[2] was chosen to be paired with the ground truth. If there were two estimates of equal angular deviation, the one with the greater saliency was chosen. Once a single estimate was selected to be paired with the ground truth, all of the remaining estimates were reclassified as *unpaired*. This resulted in either a pairing between a single ground truth and a single estimate, an unpaired estimate, or an unpaired ground truth. The final error measure was calculated as per Equation 5.1 and is referred to as the *saliency-angular error*, (SAE):

$$SAE = \sum_{e=1}^{N_e} \left\{ \left[\, | s\,(e) - s\,(pair\,(e)) | + \varepsilon \right] \left[\frac{dev\,(e, pair\,(e))}{N} + \varepsilon \right] - \varepsilon^2 \right\} + \frac{1}{2} \sum_{g=1}^{N_{ug}} | s\,(g) |$$
$$(5.1)$$

$$pair\,(e) = \begin{cases} G & \text{if } e \text{ is part of a } pair \text{ with ground truth } G \\ 0 & \text{otherwise} \end{cases} \qquad (5.2)$$

where N_e is the total number of estimates, $s(...)$ returns the saliency of an individual estimate or ground truth, $dev(...)$ calculates the absolute angular difference between a pairing of indices that range from $[1, N]$ where N is the number of angular bins. The N_{ug} corresponds to the number of *unpaired ground truths* and $\varepsilon = 0.1$ to assure that neither the angular nor the saliency difference negates the influence of one another. The $\frac{1}{2}$ in the second term of the *SAE* is to represent the

---

[2]The term closest, in this step, refers to the closest angular estimate.

maximum angular difference of π, where 2π is normalized to one. In the event that $pair(e) = 0$, $s(...)$ equals zero. For further details, see Appendix B.

Although seemingly complex, these equations describing the DDF error are actually based on two simple concepts. The *SAE* gives reduced errors for estimates that are close in both saliency and angular direction to the ground truth, while DDFs with too many or too few estimates with respect to the number of ground truths have increased error values.

5.1.3   Spatial Frequency Trial

Where the previous trial exposed some of the general advantages and disadvantages of each method, the spatial frequency trial quantitatively measured the error of each method in an effort to compare the algorithms fairly. In this trial, the spatial frequency was varied uniformly for the horizontal and vertical bands of the test image. For example, in Figure 5.3b, where the spatial frequency was equal to one, exactly one period of a sine wave is visible along the vertical bands. The horizontal bands are occluded in the bottom half of the swatch. This setup was chosen to detail how convolution approaches are highly dependent on spatial frequency, and to provide an asymmetric pattern where there are no vertical edges in the top half. The ground truth model for this structure is shown in Figure 5.2a with equal saliencies for each direction.

The algorithms were applied to swatches of spatial frequencies between [0.5, 5] with 0.1 increments and their error measurements are shown in Figure 5.3d. The same set of parameters were used in this trial as those in the previous trial. The convolution approaches exhibited relatively small error values at frequency ranges coinciding with the set of parameters chosen for this experiment. If the parameters are changed, so does the frequency range that exhibits reduced error values. This effect was charted and is shown in Figure 5.4 where different frequency parameters were used for the Gabor and one-sided methods, while wedge sizes were varied for the wedge filter and RAWM. A collection of differently tuned filters is required in order to reduce error rates across all of the spatial frequencies. In this case, one must still select *which* of the DDFs best represents the local structure. Among convolution approaches, the Fourier method exhibited the smallest error measures in the range of [0.75, 2), while the Gabor and one-sided methods exhibited minimal errors above this range.

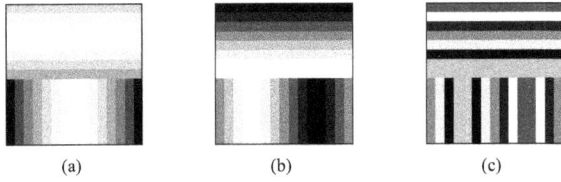

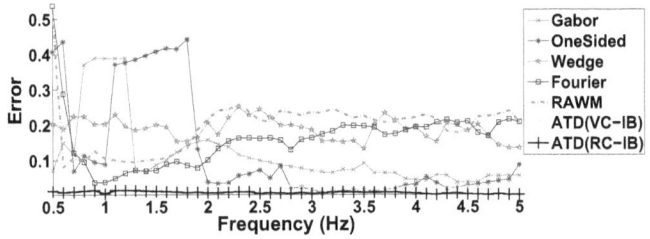

Figure 5.3: (a-c) sample T-junction swatches at $f = 0.5$, $f = 1$ and $f = 5$ respectively. (d) the graph of errors for the various methods across the frequency range of $[0.5, 5]$.

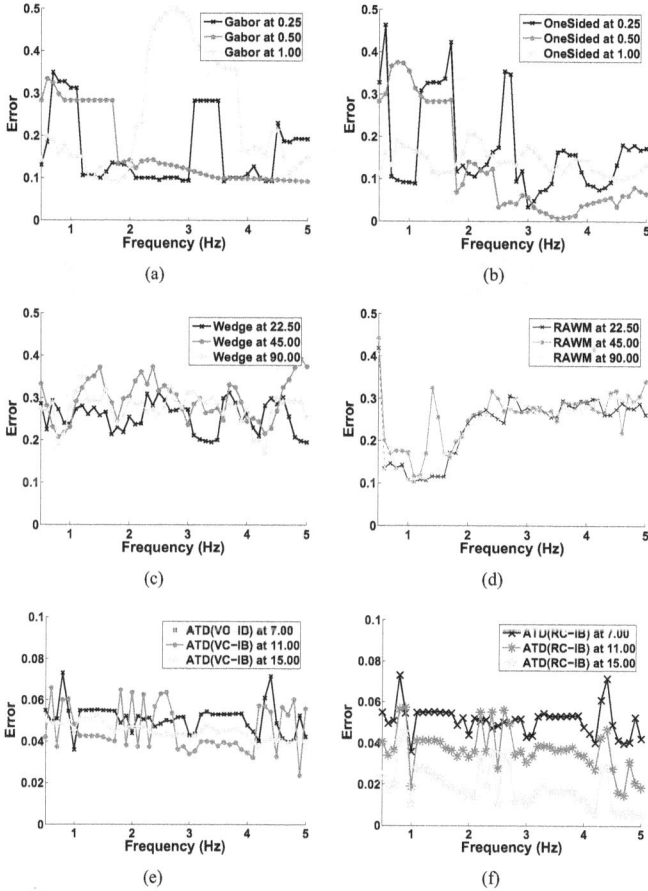

Figure 5.4: Error measures for three different parameter values for (a) frequency within the Gabor equation, (b) frequency within one-sided equation, (c) angular wedge size for the wedge filter, (d) angular wedge size for the RAWM, (e) diffusion scale of ATD (VC-IB) and (f) diffusion scale of ATD (RC-IB). *NB: The vertical axis for the ATD approaches is half an order of magnitude smaller than that used for the other methods.

	Mean	Variance
Gabor	0.057909	0.002526
one-sided	0.061074	0.005913
wedge	0.094344	0.000225
Fourier	0.079398	0.001622
RAWM	0.097215	0.001366
ATD (VC-IB)	0.009078	0.000001
ATD (RC-IB)	0.004316	0.000003

Table 5.1: Error mean and variance for the spatial frequency trial.

Both the VC-IB and RC-IB versions of the ATD exhibited consistently low error rates throughout the frequency range, as shown in Table 5.1. The ATD approaches exhibited the least mean and variance errors that illustrated their robustness to differing spatial frequencies. The change in error with different parameters was observed for three different diffusion scales, as shown in Figures 5.4(e and f). As expected, error decreased for this test case when the diffusion scale increased. This is due to the corresponding increase in the number of neighbors that cast ballots, which results in the DDFs created from a greater population. Note also that the change in error values between diffusion scales was relatively constant across spatial frequencies.[3] Larger diffusion scales, which allow a greater number of structural patterns within the ROI, may dilute more complicated structures, at least in the first iteration. It should be noted that both ATD approaches were more computationally expensive than the convolution methods, due mainly to the choice of iteration steps and diffusion scale. The tradeoff, of course, is that the ATD offered a precise depiction of the underlying gradient structure.

Sample DDFs from each of the algorithms at two different frequencies are shown in Figure 5.5. At a frequency of 0.5, only the ATD paradigms produced a DDF similar to a T-shaped structure, with corresponding low error in Figure 5.3d. The Gabor also exhibited a low error value resulting from its salient estimates along the horizontal, with lesser salient lobes along the vertical orientation. The presence of an estimate directed upwards, which resulted from the Gabor's symmetric response, increased its error in this instance. The one-sided approach, with the next least error after Gabor, had only two estimates that were similar to the horizontally directed ground truths. At the higher frequency of 5, the wedge

---

[3]The error graph has the same approximate pattern, only shifted vertically between parameter changes.

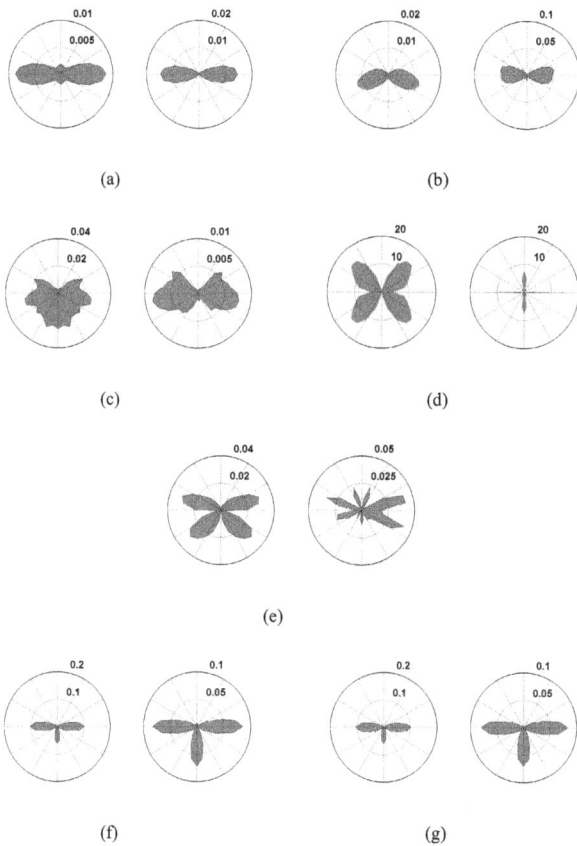

Figure 5.5: The DDFs associated with spatial frequency for $f = 0.5$ (left) and $f = 5$ (right) using (a) Gabor, (b) one-sided, (c) wedge filter, (d) Fourier, (e) RAWM, (f) ATD (VC-IB) and (g) ATD (RC-IB). The overlaid numbers in the figures denote tick marks along the radial axis.

(a)	(b)	(c)

(d)

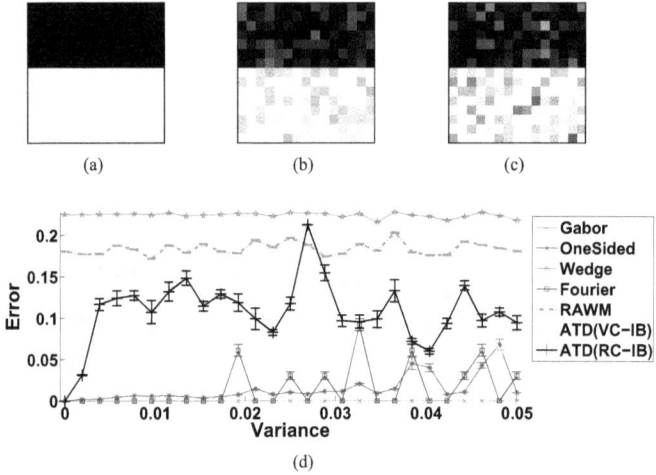

Figure 5.6: (a-c) sample images with additive Gaussian noise at variance values $(0, 0.0025, 0.05)$ respectively. (d) results of the mean error measures per algorithm with overlaid error-bars corresponding to the variance range.

filter and the RAWM, both of which use an angular wedge parameter, had difficulty isolating salient estimates. This resulted from the off-center edges in the test image. It should be noted that the Fourier approach properly identified both of the *orientations* present at this higher frequency; however, it was unable to represent the absence of vertical edges in the top-half of the image due to its symmetric nature in creating the DDF. For both frequencies, the ATD was able to identify the three, and only three, ground truth directions properly. The non-zero error of these methods results from the saliencies (lobe sizes) not being equal to those of the ground truth model.

5.1.4 Gaussian Noise Trial

The next trial was to test the robustness of the algorithms against additive Gaussian noise. The first test case used a simple horizontal step-edge image, as shown in Figure 5.6a. The ground truth was defined as two directions at $\theta = 0^o$ and $\theta = 180^o$ with equal saliency components.

	Mean	Variance
Gabor	0.000000	0.000000
OneSided	0.014152	0.000256
Wedge	0.224282	0.000009
Fourier	0.014712	0.000673
RAWM	0.183803	0.000055
ATD (VC-IB)	0.122946	0.001636
ATD (RC-IB)	0.107653	0.001586

Table 5.2: Error mean and variance for the Gaussian noise trial applied to the simulated horizontal step-edge image.

The error measures were calculated against increasing amounts of zero-mean additive Gaussian noise with a variance range of $[0, 0.05]$. The results from five different applications of Gaussian noise were combined, where the mean error formed the graph contours and the variance was depicted as error bars in Figure 5.6d.

Since the two ground truth directions also defined a single orientation (horizontal), both the Gabor and Fourier approaches performed especially well for this test case. Even with increasing amounts of noise, the Gabor approach produced satisfactory results. Both the wedge filter and RAWM performed poorly throughout, most likely resulting from the true step-edge being centered *between* pixels, thus the estimates consistently were directed slightly upwards.[4] Both the VC-IB and the RC-IB paradigms had relatively the same error graphs. The mean and variance of the error for each of these algorithms are shown in Table 5.2. For these values, the Gabor proved to be immune to the noise.

As noise was added, the convolution approaches decreased their saliencies or beliefs in their estimates resulting from the increased uncertainty. Both of the ATD approaches, however, *increased* their saliencies as noise was added. This behavior resulted from the initial calculation of the structure tensors at each pixel location with a *normalized* gradient magnitude.[5] In a simulated test case such as this one, pixels within the monochromatic regions had exactly zero gradient magnitude. This implies that there is no definitive direction with which to normalize the gradient information, hence a magnitude of zero must be used. This event is

---

[4]As the convolution kernels are applied over a discretely sampled mask of odd-dimension, the mask is never centered over the step-edge.

[5]Normalization of gradient information, in this context, refers to retaining the gradient direction, but replacing the magnitude with one.

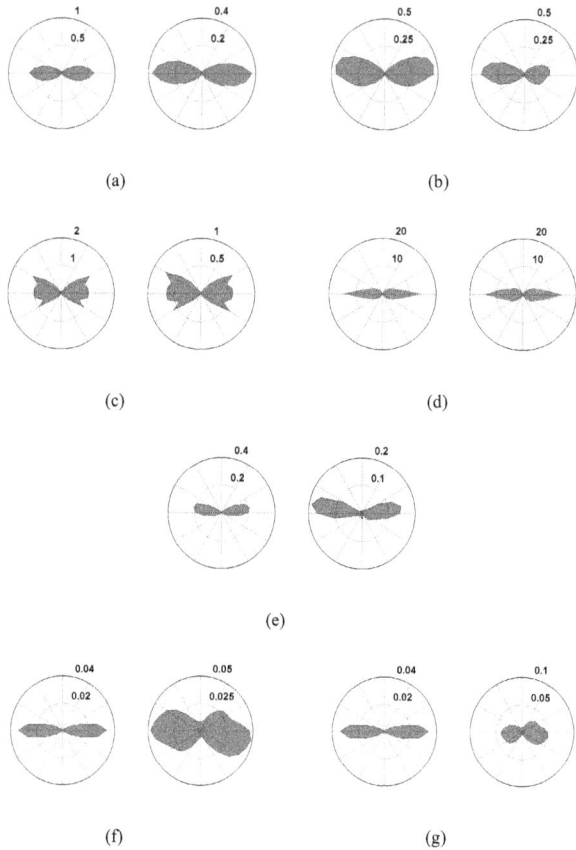

Figure 5.7: The DDF associated with no Gaussian noise (left) and Gaussian noise with variance=0.05 (right) for (a) Gabor, (b) one-sided, (c) wedge filter, (d) Fourier, (e) RAWM, (f) ATD (VC-IB) and (g) ATD (RC-IB).

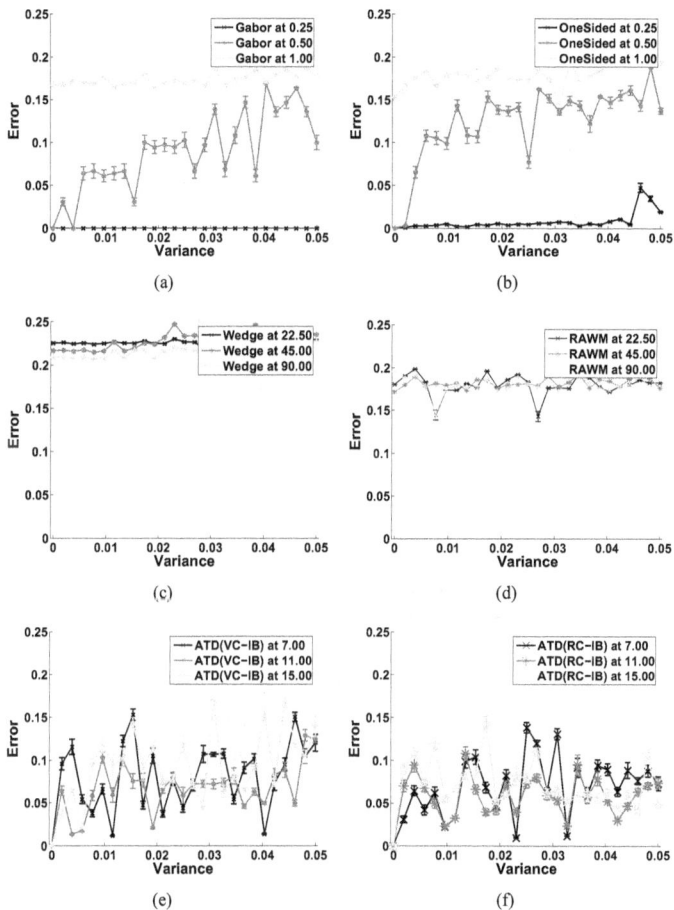

Figure 5.8: Error measures for three different parameter values for (a) frequency within the Gabor equation, (b) frequency within one-sided equation, (c) angular wedge size for the wedge filter, (d) angular wedge size for the RAWM, (e) diffusion scale of ATD (VC-IB) and (f) diffusion scale of ATD (RC-IB).

quite rare and only found with simulated cases as most real images have at least a single color-level difference between neighboring pixels to produce a non-zero gradient magnitude that can in turn be normalized to one. To prevent this pathological case, the raw gradient magnitude could be used rather than the normalized magnitude; however, normalization has the advantage of reducing the influence of noise. Although this scenario occurs infrequently, this case is presented here to illustrate one of the disadvantages of the ATD.

Changing the parameters within each of the algorithms also had a markedly different effect in this trial. As shown in Figure 5.8a, the low frequency Gabor worked well, which corresponded with the characteristics of the input image. As the Gabor frequency parameter was increased, it became more sensitive to noise. This was also observed for the one-sided method. Both the wedge filter and RAWM approaches were relatively resistant to change between the various angular wedge parameters, while both of the ATD approaches had minimal rise in the error values as the diffusion scale increased.

The next noise trial was performed using an asymmetric pattern derived from the T-junction pattern where both the top and bottom halves had a spatial frequency of 2.5, as in Figure 5.9a. The ground truth used for this experiment was the same as that used for the spatial frequency trial. With the asymmetric structure, both of the ATD paradigms exhibited the least error up to a Gaussian noise variance of approximately 0.035 as shown in Figure 5.9d. The symmetric approaches, Gabor and Fourier, had increased errors due to their inability to represent the absence of vertical direction in the top half. Both the wedge filter and RAWM approaches remained those with the highest error measures.

The error value mean and variance across all of the noise images were calculated and shown in Table 5.3. While the convolution approaches obtained lower error variances, the ATD approaches exhibited the least mean error.

Sample DDFs corresponding to the swatches of Figure 5.9a with no noise and 5.9c with Gaussian noise of variance of 0.05, are depicted in Figure 5.10. The T-junction structure was quickly lost by the wedge filter and RAWM approaches. The Fourier method, and to lesser extent the Gabor method, was adept in identifying the orientations, if not the directions. Note here the *decrease* in saliency as noise increased for the ATD methods. This is expected as the normalization effect, discussed in the step-edge trial, is no longer prevalent.

The effects of changing the parameters for this trial are shown in Figure 5.11.

| (a) | (b) | (c) |

(d)

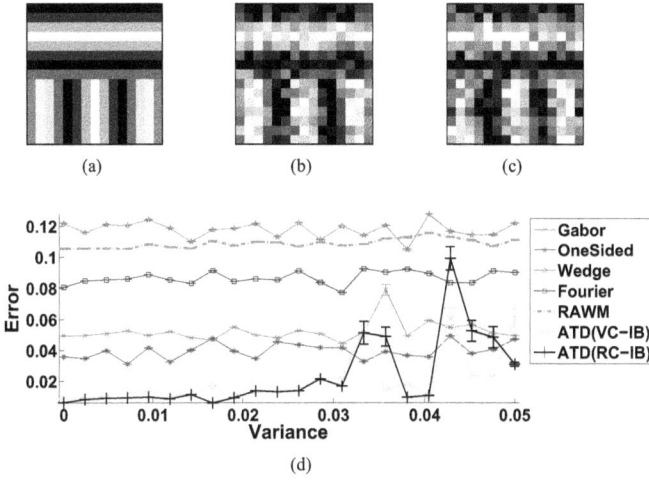

Figure 5.9: (a-c) error measures when applied against T-junction swatches with $f = 2.5$ as per the spatial frequency trial, with additive Gaussian noise at variance values $(0, 0.0025, 0.05)$ respectively. (d) results of the mean error measures per algorithm with overlaid error bars corresponding to the variance range.

	Mean	Variance
Gabor	0.052408	0.000046
OneSided	0.039668	0.000025
Wedge	0.117915	0.000027
Fourier	0.086691	0.000016
RAWM	0.108906	0.000009
ATD (VC-IB)	0.021034	0.000268
ATD (RC-IB)	0.023255	0.000542

Table 5.3: Error mean and variance for the Gaussian noise applied to the T-junction pattern.

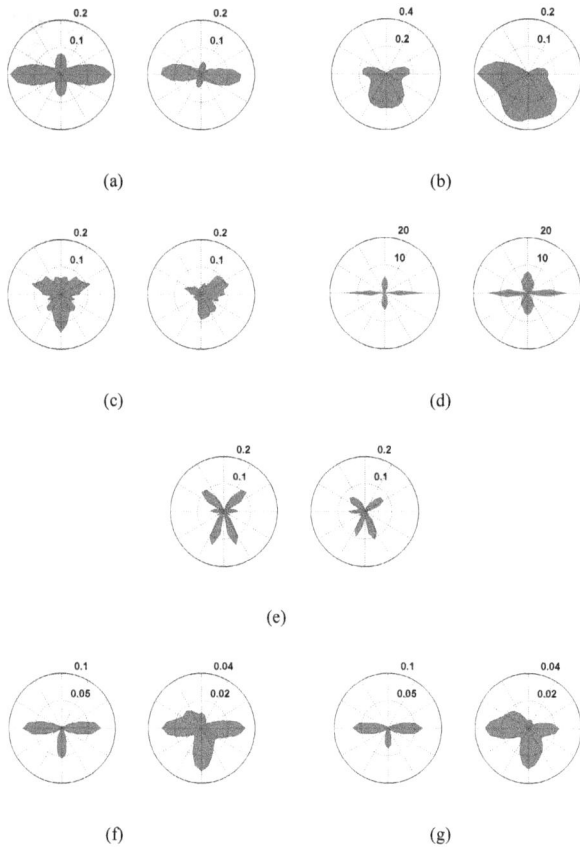

Figure 5.10: The DDFs associated with no Gaussian noise (left) and Gaussian noise with variance=0.05 (right) for (a) Gabor, (b) one-sided, (c) wedge filter, (d) Fourier, (e) RAWM, (f) ATD (VC-IB) and (g) ATD (RC-IB).

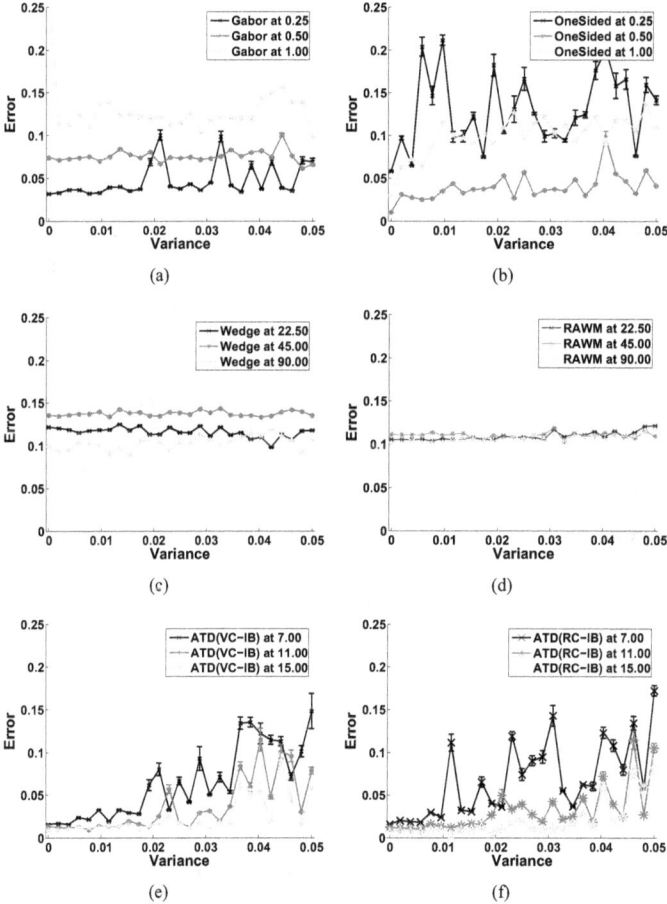

Figure 5.11: Error measures for three different parameter values for (a) frequency within the Gabor equation, (b) frequency within one-sided equation, (c) angular wedge size for the wedge filter, (d) angular wedge size for the RAWM, (e) diffusion scale of ATD (VC-IB) and (f) diffusion scale of ATD (RC-IB).

As the Gabor frequency parameter increased, the error also increased across the noise range. For the ATD approaches, the error over the entire range of noise decreased as the diffusion scale increased.

5.2   Diffusion Methods

The ATD approaches were compared with previous diffusion methods using several predefined tensor field layouts. The first test highlighted the importance of a symmetric DDF in the diffusion framework by comparing a 'T' and 'X'-shaped tensor layout. The second test examined the effects of both sparse information and three different types of noise applied to a predefined tensor field. In brief, the ATD approaches provided superior DDFs as they were capable of representing the underlying structure asymmetrically. For the noise trials, the tensor voting approach provided the most consistent junction *location* estimates in the presence of several different types of noise. These included the addition of extra samples as well as noise added to the spatial location of the original samples and to the gradient data itself. Nevertheless, the tensor voting approach was incapable of representing the junction type given its single tensor representation. The relaxation labeling approach was able to represent the orientations of the underlying junctions; however, had problems with the last noise trial, as did the ATD. Overall, the ATD approaches were the only methods able to consistently identify the asymmetric structure of end-points as well as represent curved contours.

5.2.1   Asymmetric Tensor Field Layout Trial

Figures 5.12(a and g) depict 'X' and 'T'-shaped structure tensor layouts respectively. Since the isotropic, anisotropic[6] and tensor voting schemes represent the local structural information using a single tensor, in elliptical form in Figure 5.12, it was not obvious whether their DDF represented a region of little structure, ball tensor, or from two perpendicular lines, which also produce a ball tensor. The relaxation labeling approach was able to represent the two *orientations*, although only the ATD approach was able to represent the asymmetric structure of the 'T' junction as well as the symmetric 'X' junction data.

---

[6]The anisotropic diffusion method used was based on a 2D Gaussian with $\sigma_y = \frac{1}{2}\sigma_x$.

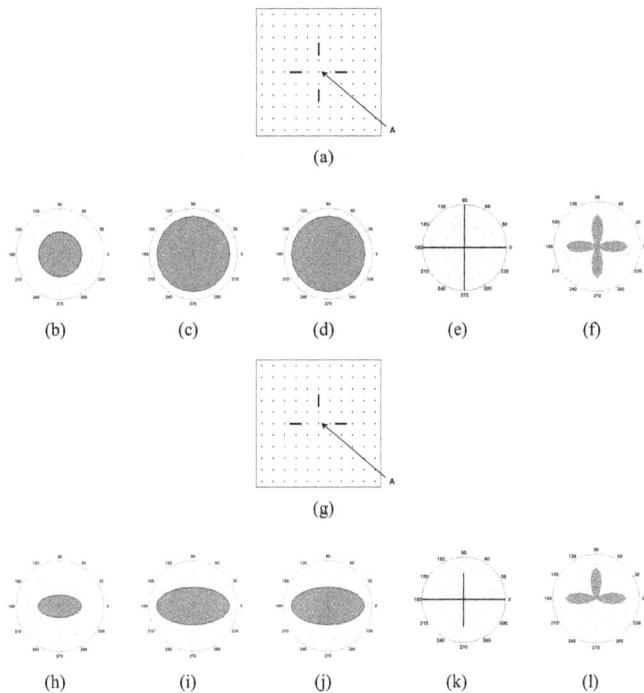

Figure 5.12: (a) X-junction tensor layout and resulting DDF at annotated location 'A' for (b) isotropic, (c) anisotropic, (d) tensor voting, (e) relaxation labeling and (f) ATD (VC-IB). (g) T-junction tensor layout and resulting DDF at annotated location 'A' for (h) isotropic, (i) anisotropic, (j) tensor voting, (k) relaxation labeling and (l) ATD (VC-IB).

85

5.2.2 Uniformly Sampled Tensor Field

A predefined tensor field was created as a ground truth benchmark to assess error accurately for the TV, RL and ATD methods. This field was constructed using a square, circle and line with junctions and overlaps as illustrated in Figure 5.13a. This particular setup was chosen as it exhibited a variety of junction types, namely a slanted 'T'-junction (A), slanted 'X'-junction (B), end-point or termination[7] (C) and symmetric 'X'-junction (D). The exact locations of these points were calculated from given the geometric parameters of the shapes. After all of the noise trials were completed, it was found that the relaxation labeling method exhibited its best estimates offset by a fixed amount from these ground truth locations for each trial. Therefore, the DDFs used to compare relaxation labeling against the remaining methods were sampled from these better estimate locations to the ground truths. It should also be noted that there was no such offset associated with the tensor voting, VC-IB or RC-IB approach. The error measurements calculated at these locations for the following experiments used the ground truth DDFs, shown in Figures 5.13(c-f) where each lobe has equal saliency.

The original tensor field was calculated by uniformly sampling points on the shapes and replacing them with stick-tensors oriented normal to the contours, as shown in Figure 5.13b. For all of the following tests, this normal-directed tensor field was used as the input for the tensor voting approach, as it was implemented in its original work [52]. The resulting DDFs were then rotated by $\frac{\pi}{2}$ for proper comparison with the remaining approaches that made use of the tangent-directed tensor field instead.

The input example had sparse contours, as opposed to a dense collection of parallel contours. Therefore, the co-circularity relaxation labeling method [60] was used rather than the right-helicoid model, which is more appropriate for regions of textural flow [9]. For all methods, the diffusion scale was 15x15 and $N = 36$. The decay function parameters for the tensor voting approach were $\sigma = 0.4$ and $c = 0.04$, which were empirically chosen. For the relaxation labeling method the seven curvature classes were the same as those used in Parent and Zucker's algorithm [60]. Both the VC-IB and RC-IB approaches used a learning coefficient of 0.5. The relaxation labeling and ATD approaches both performed

---

[7]Although an end-point is not a *junction* in the sense of the meeting of two or more edge segments. It *is* an asymmetric structure and is thus included in these results.

two iterations. All of the methods implemented dense voting.

The results of tensor voting, relaxation labeling, VC-IB and RC-IB are depicted in Figures 5.13(g-j) respectively. Close-ups of the DDFs associated with the four annotated junction locations of Figure 5.13a are shown in Table 5.4. For ease of comparison, the tensor voting DDFs were interpreted as two directional estimates along $\vec{e}_1$ and $-\vec{e}_1$. In order to avoid the impression that the *SAE* error metric was chosen deliberately to favor the ATD approach, the same comparison is made using the simpler SSD error calculation as well, as seen in Figure 5.13k. Both the VC-IB and RC-IB approaches outperformed both the tensor voting and relaxation labeling approaches at all four nodes primarily because the ATD was able to propagate structural information asymmetrically to its neighbors. The elevated error rates produced by the tensor voting approach were due to the single tensor representation of local structure as well as its DDF tending towards a ball-shaped tensor at junctions. The relaxation labeling approach gave comparable results to those of the ATD for the symmetric junctions (nodes 'B' and 'D'), but was unable to represent the asymmetry of the line-square junction ('A') and the line termination ('C').

Although the primary motivation for the ATD was to represent local structure asymmetrically, it may also work as a junction *detector*. The locations of junctions as per the tensor voting approach are depicted in first row of Table 5.5. This approach performed well in localizing the junction at node 'D' but had difficulty with the others. For the relaxation labeling and ATD approaches, the junction location maps were created by first sorting those DDFs with the same number of lobes (estimates) and then representing these locations by their respective total saliencies. The second row of Table 5.5 shows the lobe count maps for 1,2,3 and 4 lobes respectively for relaxation labeling. Since this approach was unable to produce an odd number of lobes, the corresponding one and three-lobed maps were unpopulated; however, the locations of two-lobed DDFs were quite accurate. In addition, relaxation labeling localized the 'X' junctions as well as two of the four corners of the square. However, only the ATD approaches were able to localize the end-point ('C') of the diagonal line. There also seemed to be weak three-lobed DDFs along some of the sides of the square for the ATD approaches rather than only around the line-square junction ('A'). This effect was most likely due to the presence of nearby contours aligned in different orientations. Nevertheless, the sampled DDFs were reasonable matches to their ground truth equivalents.

87

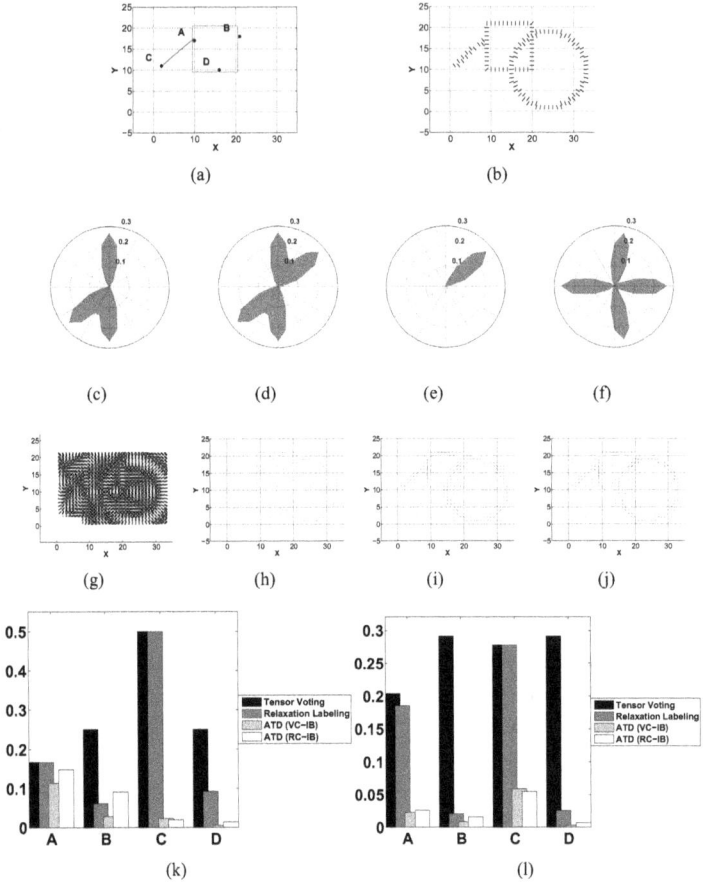

Figure 5.13: (a) group of shapes and their junctions and (b) its uniformly sub-sampled tensor field defined normal to the contours. (c-f) the ground truth representations at the four annotated nodes as per (a) at 'A','B','C','D' respectively. Results of (g) tensor voting, (h) relaxation labeling, (i) ATD (VC-IB), and (j) ATD (RC-IB). (k and l) the error calculated at the annotated nodes using SSD error and the *SAE* respectively.

88

	'A'	'B'	'C'	'D'
Ground Truth				
Tensor Voting				
Relaxation Labeling				
ATD (VC-IB)				
ATD (RC-IB)				

Table 5.4: Case 1: Comparison of the DDFs at the annotated nodes 'A','B','C' and 'D' in Figure 5.13a using (second row) tensor voting, (third row) relaxation labeling (fourth row) ATD (VC-IB) and (fifth row) ATD (RC-IB).

	Stick Saliency (TV)		Ball Saliency (TV)	
TV				
	1-lobe	2-lobe	3-lobe	4-lobe
RL				
VC-IB				
RC-IB				

Table 5.5: Case 1: Junction detection results using the stick and ball saliency for tensor voting and lobe-count maps for relaxation labeling and ATD as described in Section 5.2.2.

5.2.3 Randomly Sampled Tensor Field

In the next trial, 25% of the previous samples were randomly selected and removed from the tensor field, as shown in Figure 5.14a, to investigate the effects of sparse information of the diffusion approaches. All of the methods performed reasonably well in approximating the underlying shapes in this experiment. The error measures for this trial were in a similar proportion to those previously with the exception of node 'C', for which the relaxation labeling method provided a zero DDF. Also, as pictured in Table 5.6, the ATD approaches at node 'B' were more accurate than the other methods.

Within the junction detection maps of Table 5.7, the tensor voting approach accurately highlighted locations along the contours and again localized the junction at node 'D' with greater confidence than the rest. The relaxation labeling method properly identified the junction at node 'A' along with the 'X'-junctions and corners of the square. The ATD localized the termination point at node 'C' and the 'X' junctions were represented appropriately with four lobes. The junction at node 'A', which should be three lobes, was incorrectly labeled in this map; however, the associated DDFs highlight the fourth errant lobe pointing eastward in the first column results of Table 5.6.

5.2.4 Noise in the form of Added Samples

In this trial, the full set of samples was used from Section 5.2.2 with a further 50% added as noise with uniformly random locations and tensor properties. This is illustrated in Figure 5.15a.

The tensor voting approach performed well under these conditions as expected from its single tensor representation. With the exception of node 'C,' the relaxation labeling approach outperformed the tensor voting approach. The ATD approaches exhibited consistently less error than either of the other methods. The DDFs are shown in Table 5.8.

For the junction detection maps in Table 5.9, tensor voting localized nodes along the contours with reasonable accuracy while its junction detection map highlighted only node 'D' along with some of the corners of the square. Relaxation labeling was robust against noise in its four-lobed junction map. The addition of noise prevented the ATD approaches from isolating node 'C' as they had in previous trials. This also resulted in an increased number of lobes of each

91

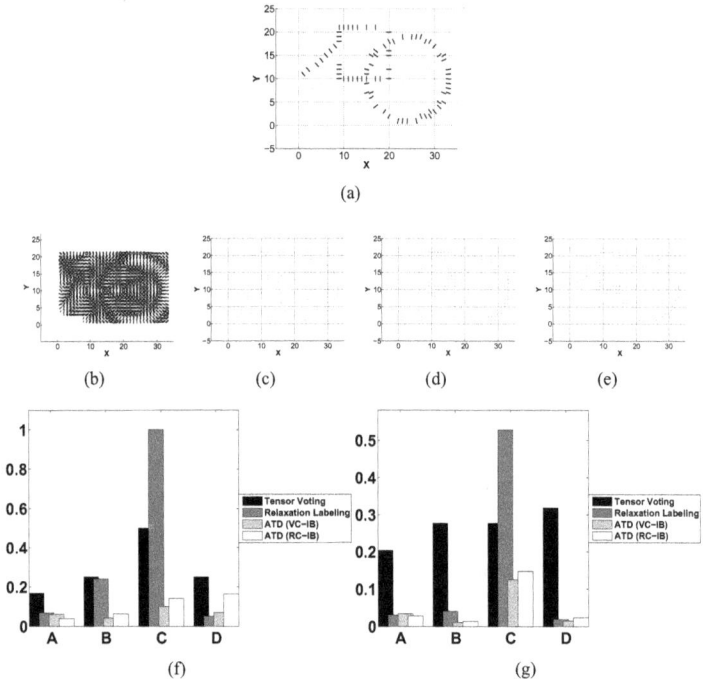

Figure 5.14: Case 2: (a) sub-sampling 25% of those points from the ground truth sampling of Figure 5.13a, (b-e) the final results for tensor voting, relaxation labeling, ATD VC-IB and RC-IB respectively. (f and g) the error calculated at the annotated nodes using SSD error and the *SAE* respectively.

	'A'	'B'	'C'	'D'
Ground Truth				
Tensor Voting				
Relaxation Labeling				
ATD (VC-IB)				
ATD (RC-IB)				

Table 5.6: Case 2: Comparison of the DDFs at the annotated nodes 'A','B','C' and 'D' in Figure 5.13a using (second row) tensor voting, (third row) relaxation labeling (fourth row) ATD (VC-IB) and (fifth row) ATD (RC-IB).

93

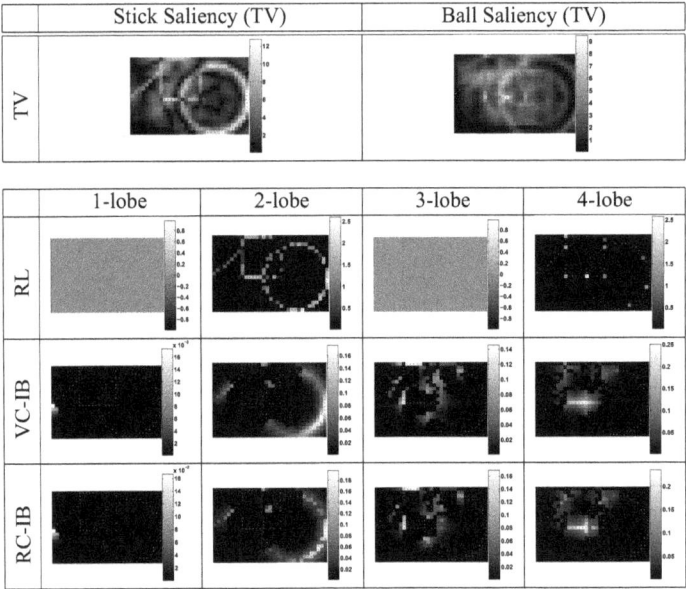

	Stick Saliency (TV)	Ball Saliency (TV)
TV		

	1-lobe	2-lobe	3-lobe	4-lobe
RL				
VC-IB				
RC-IB				

Table 5.7: Case 2: Junction detection results using the stick and ball saliency for tensor voting and lobe-count maps for relaxation labeling and ATD as described in Section 5.2.2.

94

DDF for the ATD approaches, as illustrated by the increased number of 4-lobed locations in the fourth column of Table 5.9.

5.2.5   Spatial Displacement Noise

The next trial used the entire set of original samples from Section 5.2.2 but with added noise to 50% of their spatial locations, as shown in Figure 5.16. The noise was Gaussian with $\sigma = 3$ in both x and y positions.

As shown in the error graphs of Figures 5.16 and the individual DDFs of Table 5.10, the ATD approaches exhibited far less error than either tensor voting or relaxation labeling. In terms of junction detection, tensor voting again identified regions along the contours. However, an erroneous strong junction estimate was produced in the center of the square in tcTable 5.11. The relaxation labeling method also seemed to have a greater number of junction estimates both along the circle and line as illustrated in the fourth column of Table 5.11. The ATD methods were able to discern the termination point at node 'C' and the asymmetrical junction at node 'A'.

5.2.6   Spatial Displacement and Data Noise

The final trial made use of the entire set of original samples from Section 5.2.2 with added noise both to the spatial displacement and tensor orientation as shown in Figure 5.17. This particular combination of noise types had some unusual effects on the results. For example, at node 'A', where the line meets the square, the error from tensor voting is comparable to those of the ATD methods. This is because the ATD approaches exhibit an eastward estimate but not a downward estimate. It is important to note the error effects at node 'B' for both the SSD error as well as the *SAE*. Using the SSD measure, relaxation labeling obtains a small error by virtue of its many estimates, as shown in Figure 5.12f whereas the RC-IB clearly has three lobes with only two similarly aligned with the ground truth. The *SAE* is able to address these concerns and as such, produces a higher error value for relaxation labeling.

Even though node 'D' was really the only consistently identified junction in the detection maps, tensor voting proved reliable in identifying isolated contours under a variety of noise scenarios. The number of DDFs with four lobes for the

95

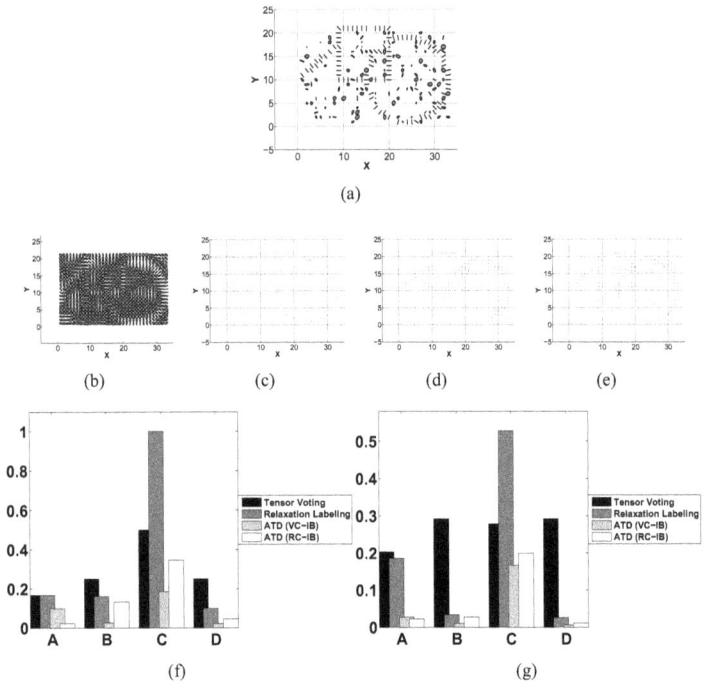

Figure 5.15: Case 3: (a) sub-sampling 50% of those points from the ground truth sampling of Figure 5.13a and adding noise in the form of extra data points, (b-e) the final results for tensor voting, relaxation labeling, ATD VC-IB and RC-IB respectively. (f and g) the error calculated at the annotated nodes using SSD error and the *SAE* respectively.

	'A'	'B'	'C'	'D'
Ground Truth				
Tensor Voting				
Relaxation Labeling				
ATD (VC-IB)				
ATD (RC-IB)				

Table 5.8: Case 3: Comparison of the DDFs at the annotated nodes 'A','B','C' and 'D' in Figure 5.13a using (second row) tensor voting, (third row) relaxation labeling (fourth row) ATD (VC-IB) and (fifth row) ATD (RC-IB).

	Stick Saliency (TV)	Ball Saliency (TV)
TV		

	1-lobe	2-lobe	3-lobe	4-lobe
RL				
VC-IB				
RC-IB				

Table 5.9: Case 3: Junction detection results using the stick and ball saliency for tensor voting and lobe-count maps for relaxation labeling and ATD as described in Section 5.2.2.

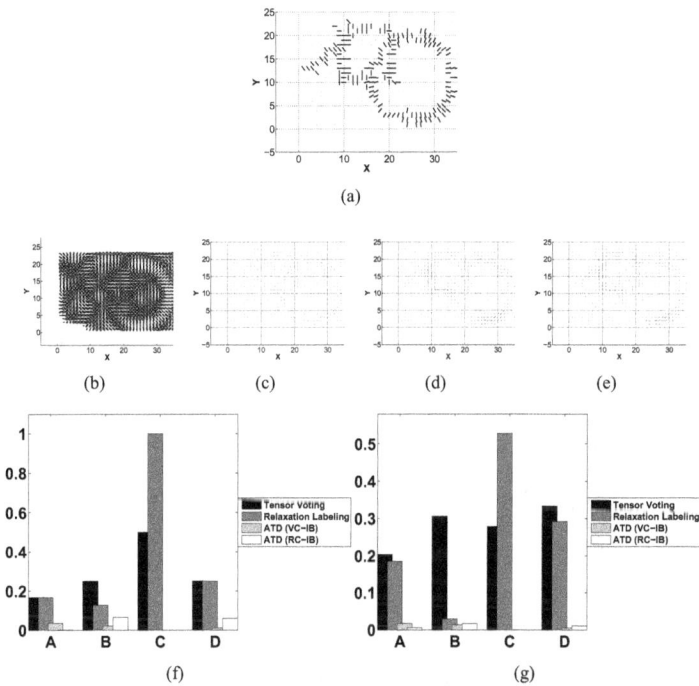

Figure 5.16: Case 4: (a) sub-sampling 50% of those points from the ground truth sampling of Figure 5.13a and adding noise in the form of spatial displacement, (b-e) the final results for tensor voting, relaxation labeling, ATD VC-IB and RC-IB respectively. (f and g) the error calculated at the annotated nodes using SSD error and the *SAE* respectively.

Table 5.10: Case 4: Comparison of the DDFs at the annotated nodes 'A','B','C' and 'D' in Figure 5.13a using (second row) tensor voting, (third row) relaxation labeling (fourth row) ATD (VC-IB) and (fifth row) ATD (RC-IB).

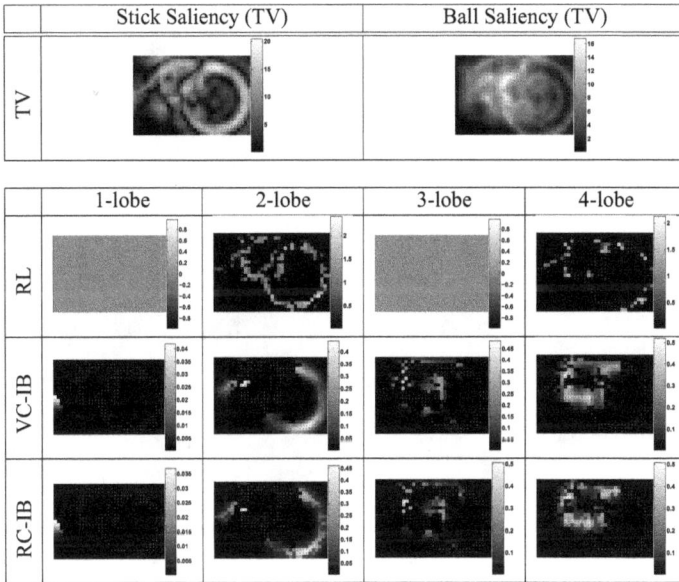

	Stick Saliency (TV)	Ball Saliency (TV)
TV		

	1-lobe	2-lobe	3-lobe	4-lobe
RL				
VC-IB				
RC-IB				

Table 5.11: Case 4: Junction detection results using the stick and ball saliency for tensor voting and lobe-count maps for relaxation labeling and ATD as described in Section 5.2.2.

relaxation labeling approach has greatly increased for the final trial although it was still adept in localizing regions along the contours. The ability of the ATD approaches to localize a single three-lobed junction is far from satisfactory in the last trial; however, they identified the termination point at node 'C' consistently throughout the rest of the experiments.

(a)

(b)   (c)   (d)   (e)

(f)   (g)

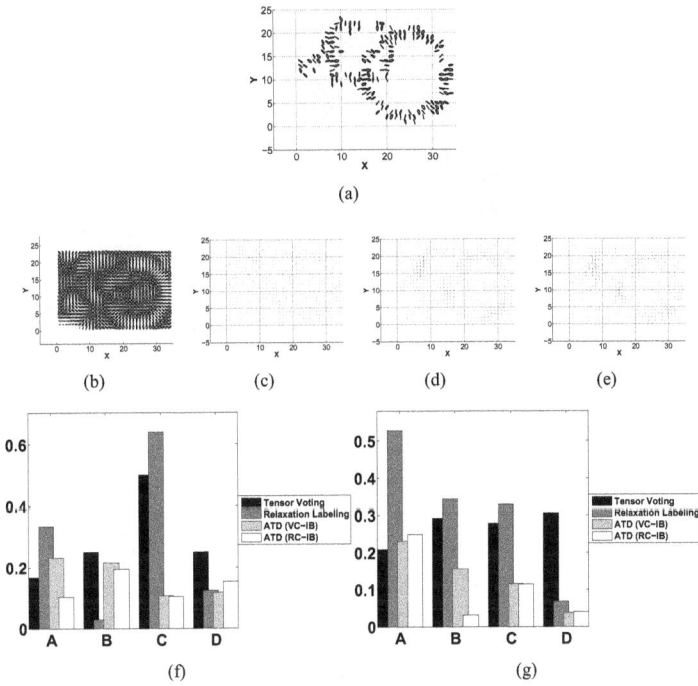

Figure 5.17: Case 5: (a) sub-sampling 50% of those points from the ground truth sampling of Figure 5.13a and adding noise to both spatial location and to the gradient data, (b-e) the final results for tensor voting, relaxation labeling, ATD VC-IB and RC-IB respectively. (f and g) the error calculated at the annotated nodes using SSD error and the *SAE* respectively.

Table 5.12: Case 5: Comparison of the DDFs at the annotated nodes 'A','B','C' and 'D' in Figure 5.13a using (second row) tensor voting, (third row) relaxation labeling (fourth row) ATD (VC-IB) and (fifth row) ATD (RC-IB).

	Stick Saliency (TV)	Ball Saliency (TV)
TV		

	1-lobe	2-lobe	3-lobe	4-lobe
RL				
VC-IB				
RC-IB				

Table 5.13: Case 5: Junction detection results using the stick and ball saliency for tensor voting and lobe-count maps for relaxation labeling and ATD as described in Section 5.2.2.

Chapter 6

Application Domains

The ATD approach is relevant to several application domains, in particular to those that require asymmetric representations of junctions. The following sections detail the results of performing the asymmetric tensor diffusion approach on several *junction analysis* applications.

6.1 Junction Analysis

The *classification* of asymmetric junctions is prevalent in many vision domains. For example, medical imaging junction analysis is applied to differentiate between branching and crossing fiber tracts in the brain using diffusion MRI data [7,72]. In fingerprint analysis, distinguishing between junction types increases the accuracy of biometric identification while in the lumber industry it is used to automate defect detection in cut timber [36,74]. The latter two applications are described in further detail in the following sections.

6.1.1 Fingerprint Analysis

The ATD is applied to the fingerprint image in Figure 6.1a to detect and classify key structural junctions. A subsection of the original image is used, shown in Figure 6.1b, such that the results can be visualized at an appropriate scale. First, the image data is transformed into a tensor field using structure tensors, which are super-imposed onto the subsection as shown in Figure 6.1c. The ATD VC-IB approach is used with the following parameters: a learning coefficient of 0.5 and a diffusion scale of 15x15 for two iterations.

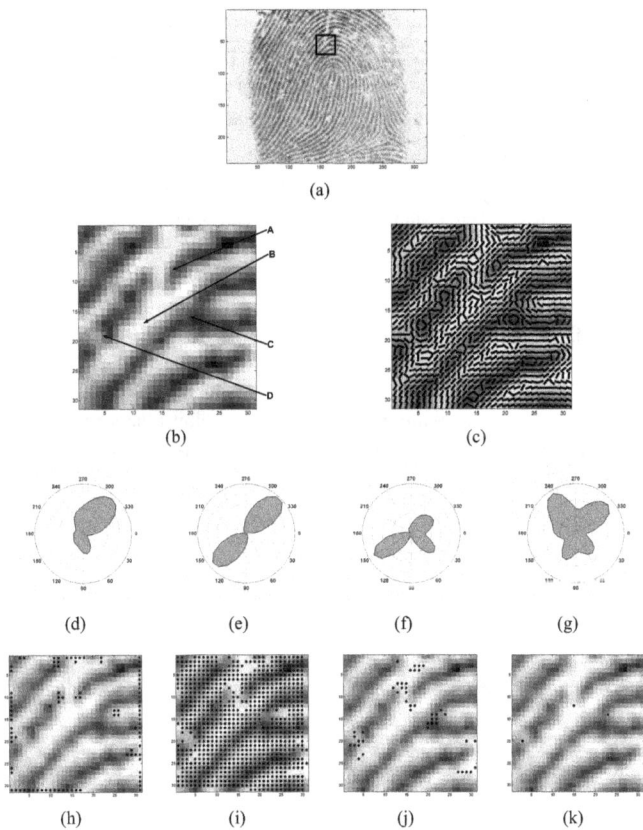

Figure 6.1: (a) fingerprint image and (b) a subsection located at the black square in (a), (c) initial gradient information, (d-g) the results of ATD at annotation 'A', 'B', 'C' and 'D' from (b) respectively, (h-k) junction classification for 1-lobes, 'L' or 2-lobes, 'T' or 3-lobes and 'X' or 4-lobes respectively.

A simple junction model, where a junction is defined by the number of distinct radial lobes, was designed as a proof-of-concept to classify each of the DDFs. Both the direction and saliency (area) of each lobe are used to form a directional estimate. Any estimate with less than 10% of the maximum saliency in the DDF is eliminated. The classes were defined for lobes with one-, two-, three- and four-lobed DDFs and are shown in Figures 6.1(h-k) respectively. Select DDFs are also shown in Figures 6.1(d-g) that correspond to the annotated nodes identified in Figure 6.1b. The structure of the DDFs mimic the underlying patterns of the fingerprint ridges. More importantly, the detection of asymmetric junctions are localized, in particular 'T'-junction and ridge end-points, which could improve fingerprint recognition results.

6.1.2 Defect Detection in Lumber

The field of *dendroclimatology*[1] is a more challenging realm than fingerprint analysis as the rings are non-uniformly spaced and exhibit a larger range of color variations [74]. Although pertinent to the study of the Earth's climate change, the more immediate use of junction detection is to identify wood-based defects, such as knots and fungus, for the lumber industry. Figure 6.2 shows the presence of a knot and the result of applying the trivial junction classification previously described in Section 6.1.1. The location of the three-lobed DDF with maximum saliency is overlaid in Figure 6.2b identifying where the 'Y'-shaped region is most salient.

A close-up of the DDFs immediately surrounding this location demonstrates that the asymmetric DDF representation is able to depict both the curved outline of the knot as well as the intersection of a tree ring and the outer ring of the knot.

6.2   Occlusion Detection

To parse or summarize a complex video sequence involves such real-world issues as lighting variations, noise, camera jitter as well as the presence of complex textures. Motion cues tend to have a higher degree of robustness than other scene features such as color, shape and texture. For applications such as target tracking

---

[1]Dendroclimatology is the study of climate change through the analysis of tree rings.

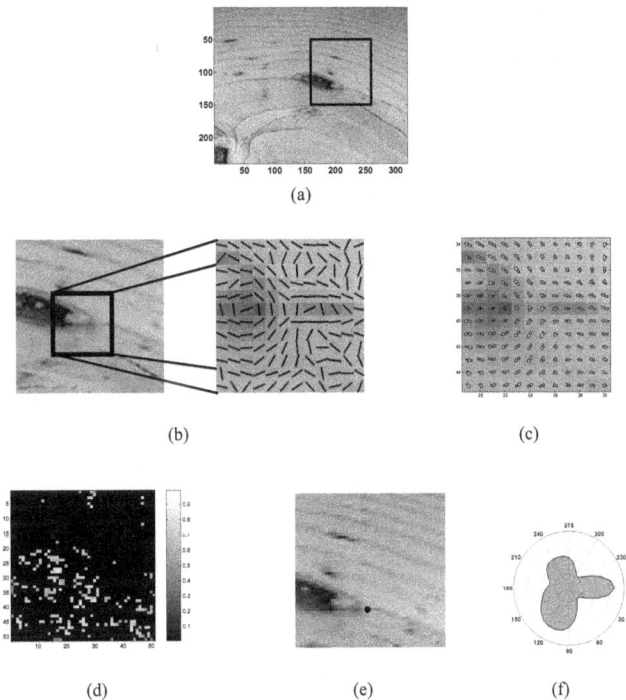

Figure 6.2: (a) sample tree cross-section image and (b) a sub-image located at the black square in (a) along with a close-up of the initial gradient information. (c) resulting DDFs after applying ATD, (d) saliency map of 3-lobed DDF from (c), (e) the DDF of maximum saliency is overlaid with a black circle. (f) the DDF at the maximum saliency location.

and ordinal depth determination, *kinetic occlusionary cues*, hereafter referred to simply as *occlusion*, provide a powerful solution for these tasks [16,59,66].

6.2.1 Previous Methods

Occlusion detection is most naturally associated with motion estimation and segmentation. Ideally, once estimates of local motions are calculated and grouped, the boundaries between such regions should coincide with occlusion.[2] This is known as a global-based occlusion detection method. In order to achieve reasonable estimates of the aforementioned motion models, many algorithms impose the single-motion constraint to local regions-of-interest such that motion boundaries can be extrapolated later in the process [6,15,56]. Bergen et al. investigated how to relax the above constraint through the iterative estimation of two underlying models; however, the approach required *a priori* knowledge of the *combining factor*[3] [10]. Irani et al. also addressed both transparency and occlusion within a video sequence [33]. Their approach was able to extract pertinent motion information without imposing the single-motion constancy constraint. This was accomplished by calculating the temporal integration that was formed by averaging a sequence of motion-warped images. Their algorithm worked well particularly in the presence of camera jitter, which is an often overlooked challenge when dealing with real-world video. Others attempted to reduce the effects of outliers in motion estimation by applying a robust operator [11], grouping regions of similar motion characteristics [20] and implementing an automatic scale-parameter calculation [73].

Identification of occlusion is not guaranteed by motion estimation techniques, as their results are dependent on how well the scene motion matches the assumed model. If the motion is more complex, or if there are many instances of simpler motion models that cannot be handled by these global-based approaches, segmentation across the motion boundaries becomes blurred or erratic. Errors in occlusion identification occur from assuming that the video sequence has only rigid-type motion, or affine or projective models [10,11,20,33]. In addition, many of the motion estimation techniques tend to either ignore or diminish the effects of

---

[2]Transparency is also possible, but the focus of this discussion is specifically on the feature of occlusion.

[3]The combining factor refers to whether the motion boundary resulted from transparency or occlusion.

occlusion to facilitate the model estimations [6, 15, 56]. Also, modeling occlusion as any sub-region in the image that disagrees with the assumed motion model is too general. For example, such sub-regions may be a result of noise or non-rigid motion within the scene [73]. The more fundamental issue with occlusion detection techniques, based on motion estimation, is that they apply a global-based approach. Therefore, further investigation into local-based approaches, such as many optical flow and orientation analysis algorithms use, is warranted.

6.2.2   Spatio-Temporal Domain

Occlusion is characterized by the presence of two motion models within a local sub-region in the spatio-temporal domain.[4] Transparency is characterized by both motion models covering the entire sub-region, whereas occlusion exhibts a distinct spatial boundary *between* the motions. Although there is some debate in the psychophysical realm as to whether junction analysis is a reasonable precursor to occlusion detection [51], it has been well established in the computer vision literature that the presence of an occlusionary event in the spatio-temporal domain appears as either a merging or splitting of temporal contours resulting in a junction pattern ⌊14, 56, 59, 78⌋. For example, the spatio-temporal volume for the well-known *flower garden* sequence is formed and a slice is extracted along $y = 80$, which is illustrated in Figures 6.3(c and e) respectively. By following along the positive time-axis of the slice image, splits or bifurcations of contours typically, but not exclusively, denote disocclusion while a merging of contours denotes occlusion.

The junctions that indicate occlusion can be observed by extracting a *spatio-temporal slice*, as shown in Figure 6.3e. Occlusion, disocclusion and the *single motion* event occur at markers 'A','B' and 'C' in Figure 6.3e, respectively. Using occlusion detection as a precursor to motion-based segmentation within the spatio-temporal framework removes the need for *a priori* knowledge of the objects' structures within the scene [42].

---

[4]The spatio-temporal domain is represented by an image sequence where the images are placed successively along the time axis forming a 3D volume.

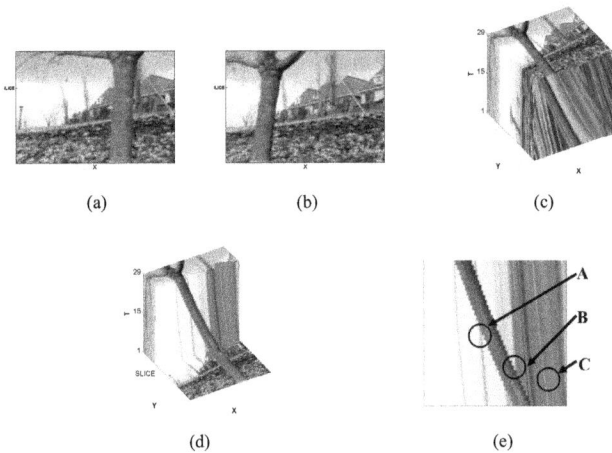

Figure 6.3: (a and b) sample images from the *flower garden* sequence at $t = 1$ and $t = 29$ respectively, (c) the spatio-temporal volume created by this sequence. (d) spatio-temporal slice is created by slicing this volume at $y = 80$ and (e) 2D view of the slice with annotated sub-regions denoting occlusion 'A', disocclusion 'B' and a single motion 'C'.

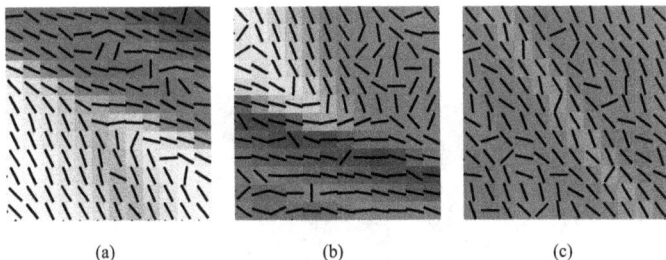

(a)   (b)   (c)

Figure 6.4: (a-c) the initial gradient information from swatch locations 'A', 'B' and 'C' of the spatio-temporal slice depicted in Figure 6.3e.

6.2.3 2D-Occlusion Detection Results

A spatio-temporal slice is extracted and the diffusion algorithms are applied to the flower garden sequence. Close-ups of the annotated locations of Figure 6.3d with the initial structure tensors superimposed appear in Figures 6.4(a-c) respectively. Each of the occlusion detection techniques use different criteria to identify and classify the junctions. For example, tensor voting uses the location of local maxima in the ball saliency fields to denote junctions while DDFs with four lobes are identified for relaxation labeling. The ATD approaches use the location of three-lobed DDFs to identify the junctions. Since the ATD DDFs are based on asymmetric information, which makes them more versatile, occlusion and disocclusion can be discerned by noting the direction of the lobe that has no symmetric pair. For example, this third lobe will either point along the positive time axis, which denotes disocclusion, or along the negative time axis, which corresponds to occlusion. To reduce run-time, the original gradient information is thresholded such that gradient magnitudes with less than 10% of the maximum gradient of the image are removed. All of the methods used a scale of 9x9 and ATD and relaxation labeling method used two iterations.

Table 6.1 illustrates close-ups of the final results of each of the diffusion methods. Although tensor voting has low computational complexity, the classification of junctions by isolating the ball tensors with local maximum saliency provides too many false positives as shown in Figure 6.5. Furthermore, since a single tensor can only model two *orthogonal* gradient directions, it is incapable of representing the asymmetric nature of occlusion. The relaxation labeling results shown in Ta-

113

Table 6.1: Diffusion results using tensor voting, relaxation labeling, ATD-VCIB and ATD-RCIB against the garden sequence slice from Figure 6.3e. Each column corresponds to close-ups of the local structures centered about swatch locations 'A', 'B' and 'C' respectively. The results are depicted in single tensor form (tensor voting) and in DDF form (relaxation labeling and ATD) overlaid on the original image.

Table 6.2: Diffusion results using tensor voting, relaxation labeling, ATD-VCIB and ATD-RCIB against the garden sequence slice from Figure 6.3e where the center structure from Table 6.1 is illustrated in greater detail.

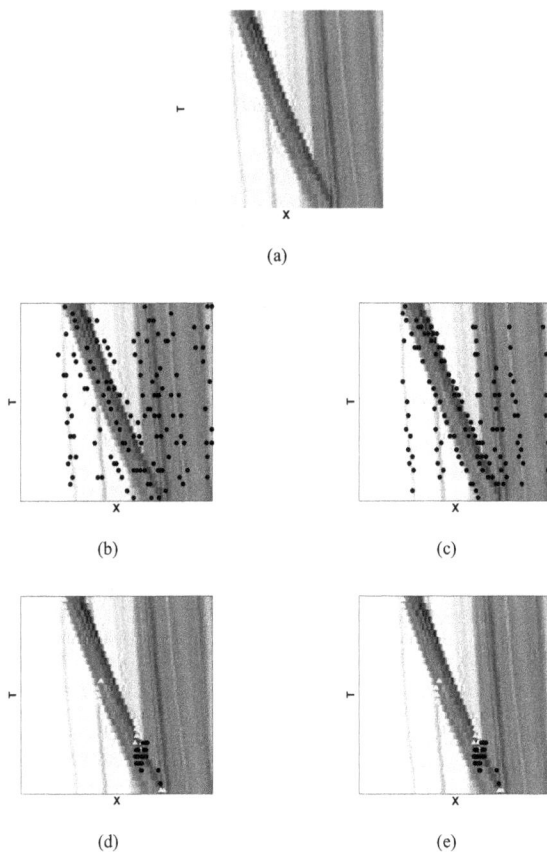

(a)

(b)   (c)

(d)   (e)

Figure 6.5: (a) Sample spatio-temporal slice from the flower garden sequence, results from (b) tensor voting, (c) relaxation labeling, (d) ATD-VCIB and (e) ATD-RCIB. The black circles in (b) and (c) denote generic junction locations whereas in the ATD results of (d) and (e) they denote disocclusion while the triangles represent occlusion.

ble 6.1 correctly mimic the alignment of the underlying gradient information of the image; however, for this instance, did not represent the local junction with two orientations as illustrated in Table 6.2. Both the VCIB and the RCIB approaches of the ATD are able to model the asymmetric nature of occlusion correctly as well as distinguish between occlusion and disocclusion by noting the direction of the lobe that has no symmetric pair. For example, for the ATD-VCIB results in Table 6.2, first column, the three-lobed DDF shows a downward pointing lobe along with two lobes that are approximately the symmetric pair of one another. Since the third lobe faces downward, this is indicative of occlusion, given that the positive time axis is directed upwards. This basic model is used as a proof of concept in Figure 6.5 where occlusion and disocclusion results are overlaid onto the original spatio-temporal slice using triangles and circles respectively.

The DDF could be useful in a preprocessing step for motion estimation or tracking by identifying locations of occlusion. However, a more powerful model for occlusion is necessary as the simple model used previously does not properly distinguish between three-lobed junctions present in the DDFs when applied to real-world images. The reason for this is that occlusion modeled as junctions in a 2D XT-slice requires that the motion in the image be strictly along the x-axis. Otherwise, image features that move in or out of the row of pixels used to create the slice, which corresponds to $y = 80$ in this example, form junctions that are not necessarily indicative of occlusion. This implies that the issue of occlusion detection is better addressed in the 3D domain.

6.2.4   3D-Occlusion Detection

Occlusion detection becomes much more complicated in the 3D domain. Rather than intersections of contours, one must contend with surfaces intersecting with other curves or surfaces. In more general terms, the conditions that depict occlusion in a 3D spatio-temporal volume must be constrained. Kinetic-based occlusion is defined as the event of one object moving in front of another with respect to the camera's viewing angle. In terms of an image sequence, occlusion occurs when a salient feature from the occluding object moves in front of a salient feature from the background. This observation facilitates a great simplification in the 3D model for occlusion.

Just as motion boundaries of objects were depicted as contours in a spatio-temporal slice, these same motion boundaries now consist of a surface in the spatio-temporal domain. Occlusion can be specified as the exact point in time when the motion boundary of the object begins to move in front of the salient background feature. This implies that occlusion occurs at the point of intersection between, for example, a surface defined by the object's boundary, and a spatio-temporal curve formed from the background feature. The key is that occlusion tends to create a *new* spatio-temporal curve, although occlusion is not the exclusive creator of such curves. This means that by identifying termination points of these 3D curves, one can identify likely points of occlusion in an image sequence. Table 6.3 illustrates several sample image sequences that depict scenarios exhibiting spatio-temporal curves. Excluding termination points of curves coincident with the first or last image of a sequence, the starting or ending of a 3D curve has a high likelihood of indicating occlusion. Both the first two columns of Table 6.3 indicate a curve through either a textural cue or an object boundary. The third and fourth columns depict the *creation* of a curve and are indicative of occlusion. One of the exceptions to this rule is shown in the fifth column where an object moves with non-rigid motion and begins to crease, which creates a spatio-temporal curve even though occlusion has not occurred.

To identify such 3D curve termination points, an antipodal approach[5] could be applied that notes the response between two angular bins that have opposite directions through the center of a sphere. This antipodal approach has many similarities with its asymmetry, its 2D counterpart.

---

[5]Antipodal refers to two points that are situated on opposite sides of a sphere such that the distance between these two points is equal to the diameter of the sphere.

Table 6.3: Sample images from sequences that either have a 3D curve throughout or create one within the spatio-temporal volume. The overlaid dashed-circle denotes the spatial location of the 3D curve in the spatio-temporal domain. First column: textural cue indicating a curve, second column: object boundary indicating a curve, third column: occlusion from zero to one to two curves, fourth column: occlusion from one to two curves, and the fifth column: crease creation that causes a curve.

119

Chapter 7

Conclusion

The proposed *asymmetric tensor diffusion* (ATD) method allows asymmetric junctions to be incorporated into the diffusion framework through a two-step process. First, the symmetric gradient information, in structure tensor representation, is transformed into asymmetric contour estimates using a voting field. This field is used to distribute data to neighboring nodes in the form of ballots. These ballots, in tensor form, are weighted based on the orientation of the original gradient data as well as the proximity to the center of the voting field. Next, the weighted ballots are propagated from the original location, known as the voter, to the neighboring locations, referred to as the receivers, using an iterative update approach. The ballots are collected into discrete angular bins at the receivers that form directional distribution functions (DDF). To account for discretization errors, linear interpolation of the populated angular bins is used to fill in the empty bins. A 2D weighting map is then constructed based on both proximity and the DDF shape characteristics. Finally, the weighting map, in conjunction with the DDF, is used to create a new voting field for the next iteration. The iterative update approach provides an appropriate local structural estimate capable of representing both symmetric and asymmetric junctions.

Several different design choices are examined for the ATD approach. For example, it is found that the inward, as opposed to the DDF, ballot form enforces co-nodal properties as well as reduces noise. The inward ballot form also decreases the amount of data being transferred from one location to another. The motivation for choosing a parallel, rather than an inward, directed voting field for the first stage of the ATD is justified by reducing the initial biasing of the data as well as simplifying the estimates of the underlying structure. A novel method is proposed that transforms the tensor-based DDF into a one dimensional DDF in order to create the DDF-based weighting map for the second stage. The benefit of a weighting map based on the local DDF properties, rather than an isotropic weighting scheme, is shown to have better diffusion results, based on the concepts of continuity and closure. In addition, two voting approaches, voter- and receiver-centered, are investigated that proved beneficial in populating among sparse data and reducing the effects of noise. It was observed that the voter-centered approach tends to address outliers by adapting them into a structural representation that agrees with the rest of its neighbors while the receiver-centered approach reduces the saliency of outlier nodes. A novel error metric is proposed that provides an improved measure of the difference between DDFs and their ground truths for use in junction analysis.

The ATD approach is compared against several convolution methods including the rotated averaging wedge method (RAWM), a Fourier-based technique as well as Gabor, one-sided and wedge filters. Results from differing angular increments for the DDF show that as the increment increases, the Gabor, Fourier, one-sided filter, as well as the ATD approach, give rise to smoother versions of the DDF while the RAWM and the wedge filter exhibit increasing numbers of local maxima. Next, the effects of Gaussian noise and spatial frequency on the directional estimates of the DDF are examined. For each of these tests, the methods are analyzed as a function of their respective tuning parameters. The results show that the ATD approach offers more flexibility and improved directional gradient estimates than those of the convolution techniques.

Next, the ATD approach is evaluated against diffusion methods. First, a simulated tensor field is used to illustrate the different representations created from isotropic diffusion, anisotropic diffusion, tensor voting, relaxation labeling and the ATD approach against a symmetric and asymmetric layout. Next, tensor voting, relaxation labeling, and two versions of the ATD approach are compared using five different tensor fields created from simulated data. Four of these trials incorporate different forms of noise such as spatial displacement and the addition of extra noise points. The DDF formed from the ATD method are shown to have superior results for a variety of scenarios including sparse data, noise as well as dense gradient information. It is versatile in that it can be applied both to a scalar field, such as an image, or to a tensor field. Finally, it is the only diffusion technique that accounts for asymmetric structures.

Several real-world applications are examined that require both the identification and classification of asymmetric junctions. For example, the ATD method is used on a fingerprint image to identify the location of both symmetric and asymmetric junctions as well as contour end-points. Also, a defect detection application is proposed that locates imperfections in lumber. The role of asymmetric junctions in occlusion detection is also examined. By noting the DDF characteristics from a spatio-temporal slice, kinetic-based occlusion can be identified in a video sequence. Tensor voting, relaxation labeling and two forms of the ATD approach are used to both identify and classify occlusion. Only the ATD approaches are capable of distinguishing between occlusion and disocclusion as they are the only methods that incorporate asymmetric information. Also, localization of occlusion within the spatio-temporal slice provides fewer false positives using the ATD methods. A 3D occlusion model based on the identification of asymmetric contour end-point structures is also proposed.

With the added flexibility of representing both symmetric and asymmetric junctions provided by the ATD approach, proper structures can be inferred for interpolation algorithms. Also, improved junction classification results from the more accurate information. Since it is an iterative update approach, only those structural estimates that indicate strong consensus are maintained while those that do not are eliminated as outliers. This not only adds a noise suppression element to the algorithm, but also reinforces local certainty measures as to the presence of various types of structures. Also, by using the structure tensor form in the first stage of the ATD, a more powerful representation of the underlying gradient structure is propagated into the final results. Lastly, the voting field design in the first stage of ATD facilitates the creation and/or maintenance of asymmetric junctions.

7.1 Future Work

The DDFs generated by the ATD have potential in application domains where the input is sparse and noisy, and depicts an underlying structure, such as in medical imaging. For example, the DDFs could aid in segmenting between various cerebral regions in the brain or add robustness to blood vessel distinction in MRI data as suggested in the previous chapter. Also, a more accurate portrayal of structure could be achieved for 3D scene reconstruction, whether originating from laser-range data or stereo depth maps.

Furthermore, the asymmetric nature of the DDFs could improve the accuracy of applications that make indirect use of gradient-based contours. For example, the ATD has potential in image enhancement where the generated DDFs could be used as an excitatory-inhibitory map over which regions are selectively smoothed. Either in-painting[1] or super-resolution could be adapted to incorporate the asymmetrical DDFs to benefit from the closure property inherit in the ATD approach. This could be accomplished by inserting empty nodes between the known pixel values and performing a dense voting approach over the sparse data. In addition, the ATD could be used to enhance edge detection or for image editing in the contour domain [22].

Future directions of this work could examine a multi-scale version of the ATD that would automatically select the optimal scale with which to represent the underlying structure. Although this approach would be more computationally expensive, it would require less memory as each DDF would represent a different sized region, similar to a quad-tree approach. Also, the effect of adding an inhibitory portion to the ROI warrants investigation for its ability to increase the accuracy of the structural representations. This would most likely reduce the number of iterations required to converge, although, a mathematical proof is required to assure that this condition will be met. Additional investigation is also warranted in transforming the DDF information into appropriate curvature values of local contours. Further research is needed to classify the DDFs into end-points, contours, and junctions when applied to real-world images. By using the ratio of saliencies between estimates, as well as examining the relationship between neighboring DDFs, the classification results could potentially improve.

There are several application domains for which the ATD holds promise as noted previously. Possible future work could focus on creating an excitatory-inhibitory map from image gradient data that would determine the boundaries between smoothing regions. Also, further experimentation is warranted to assess the proposed 3D occlusion model. Given the locations of occlusion in the spatio-temporal domain, connected contours and surfaces could be created to segment the scene based on ordinal depth.

---

[1]In-painting refers to filling in missing blocks of pixels in an image.

Bibliography

[1] E. Adelson and J. Bergen, "Spatiotemporal energy models for the perception of motion," *Journal of the Optical Society of America*, vol. 2, pp. 284–299, 1985.

[2] R. Ariew, "Ockham's razor: A historical and philosophical analysis of Ockham's principle of parsimony," Ph.D. dissertation, University of Illinois, Champaign-Urbana, 1976.

[3] S. Arseneau and J. Cooperstock, "An asymmetrical diffusion framework for junction analysis," in *British Machine Vision Conference*, vol. 2, 2006, pp. 689–698.

[4] ——, "An improved representation of junctions through asymmetric tensor diffusion," in *International Symposium on Visual Computing*, vol. 1, 2006, pp. 363–372.

[5] D. Barash, "A fundamental relationship between bilateral filtering, adaptive smoothing and the nonlinear diffusion equation," *IEEE Trans. on Pattern Analysis and Machine Intelligence*, vol. 24, no. 6, pp. 844–847, 2002.

[6] J. Barron, D. Fleet, and S. Beauchemin, "Performance of optical flow techniques," *International Journal of Computer Vision*, vol. 12, no. 1, pp. 43–77, Feb. 1994.

[7] P. Basser, J. Matiello, and D. LeBihan, "Mr diffusion tensor spectroscopy and imaging," *Biophysical Journal*, vol. 66, pp. 259–267, 1994.

[8] O. Ben-Shahar and S. Zucker, "Hue fields and color curvatures: A perceptual organization approach to color image denoising," in *Proc. IEEE Computer Vision and Pattern Recognition*, vol. 2, 2003, pp. 713–720.

[9] ——, "The perceptual organization of texture flow: A contextual inference approach," *IEEE Trans. on Pattern Analysis and Machine Intelligence*, vol. 25, no. 4, pp. 401–417, Apr. 2003.

[10] J. Bergen, P. Burt, R. Hingorani, and S. Peleg, "A three-frame algorithm for estimating two-component image motion," *IEEE Trans. on Pattern Analysis and Machine Intelligence*, vol. 14, no. 9, pp. 886–896, 1992.

124

[11] M. Black and P. Anandan, "The robust estimation of multiple motions: Parametric and piecewise-smooth flow fields," *Computer Vision and Image Understanding*, vol. 63, no. 1, pp. 75–104, 1994.

[12] M. Black, G. Sapiro, D. Marimont, and D. Heeger, "Robust anisotropic diffusion," *IEEE Trans. On Image Processing*, vol. 7, no. 3, pp. 421–432, 1998.

[13] P. Blomgren and T. Chan, "Color tv: Total variation methods for restoration of vector-valued images," *IEEE Trans. On Image Processing*, vol. 7, no. 3, pp. 304–309, 1998.

[14] R. Bolles, H. Baker, and D. Marimont, "Epipolar-plane image analysis: An approach to determining structure from motion," *International Journal of Computer Vision*, vol. 1, pp. 7–55, 1987.

[15] P. Bouthemy, "A maximum likelihood framework for determining moving edges," *IEEE Trans. On Pattern Analysis and Machine Intelligence*, vol. 11, no. 5, pp. 499–511, 1989.

[16] G. Brostow and I. Essa, "Motion based decomposition of video," in *Proc. IEEE International Conference on Computer Vision*, vol. 1, 1999, pp. 8–13.

[17] T. Brox, J. Weickert, B. Burgeth, and P. Mrázek, "Nonlinear structure tensors," in *Universität des Saarlandes, Tech. Report #113*, 2004, pp. 1–32.

[18] F. Catté, P. Lions, J. Morel, and T. Coll, "Image selective smoothing and edge detection by nonlinear diffusion," *SIAM Journal of Numerical Analysis*, vol. 29, no. 1, pp. 182–193, 1992.

[19] W. Chen and S. Acton, "Morphological pyramids for multiscale edge detection," in *Proc. IEEE Southwest Symposium on Image Analysis and Interpretation*, 1998, pp. 137–141.

[20] T. Darrell and A. Pentland, "Cooperative robust estimation using layers of support," *IEEE Trans. on Pattern Analysis and Machine Intelligence*, vol. 17, no. 5, pp. 474–487, 1995.

[21] J. Daugman, "Uncertainty relations for resolution in space, spatial frequency, and orientation optimized by two-dimensional visual cortical filters," *Journal of the Optical Society of America A*, vol. 2, pp. 1160–1169, 1985.

[22] J. Elder and R. Goldberg, "Image editing in the contour domain," in *Proc. IEEE Computer Vision and Pattern Recognition*, 1998, pp. 374–381.

[23] J. Elder and S. Zucker, "Local scale control for edge detection and blur estimation," *IEEE Trans. Pattern Anal. Machine Intell.*, vol. 20, no. 7, pp. 699–716, 1998.

[24] W. Förstner, "A feature based correspondence algorithm for image matching," *International Archives of Photogrammetry and Remote Sensing*, vol. 26, pp. 150–166, 1986.

[25] D. Forsyth and J. Ponce, *Computer Vision: A Modern Approach.* New Jersey: Prentice Hall, 2003.

[26] W. Freeman and E. Adelson, "The design and use of steerable filters," *IEEE Trans. Pattern Anal. Machine Intell.*, vol. 13, no. 9, pp. 891–906, 1991.

[27] W. Freeman, K. Tanaka, J. Ohta, and K. Kyuma, "Computer vision for computer games," in *2nd International Conference on Automatic Face and Gesture Recognition*, 1996, pp. 100–105.

[28] G. Granlund and H. Knutsson, *Signal Processing in Computer Vision.* Dordrecht: Kluwer, 1995.

[29] G. Guy and G. Medioni, "Perceptual grouping using global saliency enhancing operators," in *Proc. IEEE International Conference on Pattern Recognition*, 1992, pp. 99–104.

[30] C. Harris and M. Stephens, "A combined corner and edge detector," in *Proc. of the 4th ALVEY Vision Conference*, 1988, pp. 147–151.

[31] D. Heeger, "Optical flow using spatiotemporal filters," *International Journal of Computer Vision*, vol. 1, no. 4, pp. 279–302, 1988.

[32] R. Hummel and S. Zucker, "On the foundations of relaxation labeling processes," *IEEE Trans. On Pattern Analysis and Machine Intelligence*, vol. 5, no. 3, pp. 267–287, May 1983.

[33] M. Irani, B. Rousso, and S. Peleg, "Computing occluding and transparent motions," *International Journal of Computer Vision*, vol. 12, no. 1, pp. 5–16, 1994.

[34] L. Iverson and S. Zucker, "Logical/linear operators for image curves," *IEEE Trans. on Pattern Analysis and Machine Intelligence*, vol. 17, no. 10, pp. 982–996, 1995.

[35] B. Jähne, *Spatio-Temporal Image Processing: Theory and Scientific Applications.* Berlin: Springer-Verlag, 1993, vol. 751.

[36] X. Jiang, "On orientation and anisotropy estimation for online fingerprint authentication," *IEEE Trans. On Signal Processing*, vol. 53, no. 10, pp. 4038–4049, 2005.

[37] F. Jurie and C. Schmid, "Scale-invariant shape features for recognition of object categories," in *Proc. IEEE Computer Vision and Pattern Recognition*, vol. 2, 2004, pp. 90–96.

[38] G. Kanizsa, *Organization in Vision: Essays on Gestalt Perception.* New York: Praeger, 1979.

[39] C. Kenney, M. Zuliani, and B. Manjunath, "An axiomatic approach to corner detection," in *Proc. IEEE Computer Vision and Pattern Recognition*, 2005, pp. 191–197.

[40] R. Kimmel, R. Malladi, and N. Sochen, "Images as embedded maps and minimal surfaces: Movies, color, texture, and volumetric medical images," *International Journal of Computer Vision*, vol. 39, no. 2, pp. 111–129, 2000.

[41] K. Koffka, *Principles of Gestalt Psychology.* New York: Harcourt, Brace & World, 1963.

[42] K. Korimilli and S. Sarkar, "Motion segmentation based on perceptual organization of spatio-temporal volumes," in *Proc. IEEE International Conference on Pattern Recognition*, vol. 3, 2000, pp. 844–849.

[43] G. Kühne, J. Weickert, O. Schuster, and S. Richter, "A tensor-driven active contour model for moving object segmentation," in *Proc. IEEE International Conference on Image Processing*, vol. 2, 2001, pp. 73–76.

[44] A. Laine, S. Schuler, J. Fan, and W. Huda, "Mammographic feature enhancement by multiscale analysis," *IEEE Trans. On Medical Imaging*, vol. 13, no. 4, pp. 725–740, 1994.

[45] T. Lindeberg, "Linear spatio-temporal scale-space," in *Proc. Scale-Space'97)*, 1997, pp. 113–127.

[46] T. Lindeberg and B. ter Haar Romeny, *Linear Scale-Space II: Early Visual Operations*, B. ter Haar Romeny, Ed. Dordrecht: Kluwer Academic Publishers, 1994.

[47] D. Lowe, "Three-dimensional object recognition from single two-dimensional images," in *Artificial Intelligence*, vol. 31, 1987, pp. 355–395.

[48] ——, "Distinctive image features from scale-invariant keypoints," *International Journal of Computer Vision*, vol. 60, no. 2, pp. 91–110, 2004.

127

[49] J. Malik, S. Belongie, J. Shi, and T. Leung, "Textons, contours and regions: Cue integration in image segmentation," in *Proc. IEEE International Conference on Computer Vision*, vol. 2, 1999, pp. 918–925.

[50] A. Massad, M. Babos, and B. Mertsching, "Perceptual grouping in grey-level images by combination of gabor filtering and tensor voting," in *Proc. IEEE International Conference on Pattern Recognition*, vol. 2, 2002, pp. 677–680.

[51] J. McDermott, "Psychophysics with junctions in real images," in *Perception*, vol. 33, 2004, pp. 1101–1127.

[52] G. Medioni, M. Lee, and C. Tang, *A Computational Framework for Feature Extraction and Segmentation.* Elsevier Science, Mar. 2000.

[53] F. Michelet, C. Germain, P. Baylou, and J. D. Costa, "Local multiple orientation estimation: Isotropic and recursive oriented network," in *Proc. IEEE International Conference on Pattern Recognition*, vol. 1, 2004, pp. 712–715.

[54] R. Mohan and R. Nevatia, "Perceptual organization for scene segmentation and description," *IEEE Trans. On Pattern Analysis and Machine Intelligence*, vol. 14, no. 6, pp. 616–635, 1992.

[55] J. Monteil and A. Beghdadi, "A new interpretation and improvement of the nonlinear anisotropic diffusion for image enhancement," *IEEE Trans. On Pattern Analysis and Machine Intelligence*, vol. 21, no. 9, pp. 940–946, 1999.

[56] C. Ngo, T. Pong, H. Zhang, and R. Chin, "Motion characterization by temporal slices analysis," in *Proc. IEEE Computer Vision and Pattern Recognition*, vol. 2, 2000, pp. 768–773.

[57] M. Nicolescu and G. Medioni, "Motion segmentation with accurate boundaries - a tensor voting approach," in *Proc. IEEE Computer Vision and Pattern Recognition*, vol. 1, 2003, pp. 382–389.

[58] ——, "A voting-based computational framework for visual motion analysis and interpretation," *IEEE Trans. Pattern Anal. Machine Intell.*, vol. 27, no. 5, pp. 739–752, 2005.

[59] S. Niyogi, "Spatiotemporal junction analysis for motion boundary segmentation," in *Proc. IEEE International Conference on Image Processing*, vol. 3, 1995, pp. 468–471.

[60] P. Parent and S. Zucker, "Trace inference, curvature consistency, and curve detection," *IEEE Trans. On Pattern Analysis and Machine Intelligence*, vol. 11, pp. 823–839, 1989.

[61] P. Perona, "Steerable-scalable kernels for edge detection and junction analysis," in *Proc. European Conference on Computer Vision*, 1992, pp. 3–18.

[62] ——, "Orientation diffusions," *IEEE Trans. On Image Processing*, vol. 7, no. 3, pp. 457–467, 1998.

[63] P. Perona and J. Malik, "Scale-space and edge detection using anisotropic diffusion," *IEEE Trans. Pattern Anal. Machine Intell.*, vol. 33, no. 7, pp. 629–639, 1990.

[64] R. Rangayyan, R. Ferrari, J. Desautels, and A. Frere, "Directional analysis of images with gabor wavelets," in *Proc. IEEE Brazilian Symposium on Computer Graphics and Image Processing*, 2000, pp. 170–177.

[65] T. Reed and H. Wechsler, "Segmentation of textured images and gestalt organization using spatial/spatial-frequency representations," *IEEE Trans. On Pattern Analysis and Machine Intelligence*, vol. 12, no. 1, pp. 1–12, 1990.

[66] Y. Ricquebourg and P. Bouthemy, "Real-time tracking of moving persons by exploiting spatio-temporal image slices," *IEEE Trans. On Pattern Analysis and Machine Intelligence*, vol. 22, no. 8, pp. 797–808, 2000.

[67] K. Rohr, "On 3d differential operators for detecting point landmarks," *Image and Vision Computing*, vol. 15, no. 3, pp. 219–233, 1997.

[68] P. Saint-Marc, J. Chen, and G. Medioni, "Adaptive smoothing: A general tool for early vision," *IEEE Trans. on Pattern Analysis and Machine Intelligence*, vol. 13, no. 6, pp. 514–529, 1991.

[69] A. Salden, B. ter Haar Romeny, L. Florack, M. Viergever, and J. Koenderink, "A complete and irreducible set of local orthogonally invariant features of 2-dimensional images," in *Proc. IEEE International Conference on Pattern Recognition*, 1992, pp. 180–184.

[70] G. Sapiro and D. Ringach, "Anisotropic diffusion of multivalued images with applications to color filtering," *IEEE Trans. on Image Processing*, vol. 5, no. 11, pp. 1582–1585, 1996.

[71] S. Sarkar, "An introduction to perceptual organization," in *IEEE International Conference on Integration of Knowledge Intensive Multi-Agent Systems*, 2003, pp. 330–335.

[72] P. Savadjiev, J. Campbell, G. Pike, and K. Siddiqi, "3d curve inference for diffusion mri regularization," in *International Conference on Medical Image Computing and Computer Assisted Intervention*, 2005, pp. 123–130.

[73] H. Sawhney and S. Ayer, "Compact representation of videos through dominant and multiple motion estimation," *IEEE Trans. on Pattern Analysis and Machine Intelligence*, vol. 18, no. 8, pp. 814–830, 1996.

[74] F. Schweingruber, *Tree Rings: Basics and Applications of Dendrochronology*. Novanet: D. Reidel Publishing Co., 1988.

[75] E. Simoncelli and H. Farid, "Steerable wedge filters for local orientation analysis," *IEEE Trans. Image Processing*, vol. 5, pp. 1377–1382, 1996.

[76] B. Tang, G. Sapiro, and V. Caselles, "Direction diffusion," in *International Conference on Computer Vision*, 1999, pp. 1245–1252.

[77] C. Tang and G. Medioni, "Curvature-augmented tensor voting for shape inference from noisy 3d data," *IEEE Trans. On Pattern Analysis and Machine Intelligence*, vol. 24, no. 6, pp. 858–864, June 2002.

[78] W. Thompson, "Structure-from-motion by tracking occlusion boundaries," in *Workshop on Visual Motion*, 1989, pp. 201–203.

[79] C. Tomasi and R. Manduchi, "Bilateral filtering for gray and color images," in *Proc. IEEE International Conference on Computer Vision*, 1998, pp. 836–846.

[80] W. Tong, C. Tang, P. Mordohai, and G. Medioni, "First order augmentation to tensor voting for boundary inference and multiscale analysis in 3d," *IEEE Trans. On Pattern Analysis and Machine Intelligence*, vol. 26, no. 5, pp. 594–611, May 2004.

[81] B. Triggs, "Detecting keypoints with stable position, orientation, and scale under illumination changes," in *Proc. European Conference on Computer Vision*, vol. 4, 2004, pp. 100–113.

[82] D. Tschumperlé and R. Deriche, "Diffusion pde's on vector-valued images," *IEEE Signal Processing Magazine*, pp. 16–25, September 2002.

[83] J. Weickert, "Anisotropic diffusion in image processing," *Ph.D Dissertation, University of Kaiserslautern, Germany*, 1996.

[84] ——, "Coherence-enhancing shock filters," *Pattern Recognition: Lecture Notes in Computer Science*, vol. 2781, pp. 1–8, 2003.

[85] W. Yu, K. Daniilidis, and G. Sommer, "Rotated wedge averaging method for junction characterization," in *Proc. IEEE Computer Vision and Pattern Recognition*, 1998, pp. 390–395.

[86] N. Zlatoff, B. Tellez, and A. Baskurt, "Image understanding and scene models: A generic framework integrating domain knowledge and gestalt theory," in *Proc. IEEE International Conference on Image Processing*, 2004, pp. 2355–2358.

Appendix A

Convergence of ATD

The following is the proof that no matter the size of the neighborhood Ω, the value for DDF_j in stage one and stage two are bounded.

A.1   Stage One

The primary equation for stage one is equation 3.7, which is re-written here for convenience:

$$DDF_j\left(\vartheta\right) = \sum_{\varepsilon=0}^{1}\sum_{i=1}^{\Omega} \tilde{S}_i \Lambda_{ij}\left(\theta_i, \varepsilon\right) match\left(\vartheta, B_{ij}\right) \qquad (A.1)$$

To force the maximum possible value for DDF_j, let each of the neighboring voters be the maximum possible gradient magnitude. Further, in order for voter i to send a ballot to angular bin ϑ of receiver j, it must be aligned with it such that either $\theta_i = \vartheta$ or $\theta_i = \vartheta + \pi$. (Given the parallel layout of the directional bin field) Also, since θ_i is derived from equation 3.2, this restricts θ_i to be equal to ϑ. Again, to maximize the votes, all neighbors are set to the maximum coherence value, which implies that the structure tensors for all of the neighbors are equal in value. This leads to the simplification:

$$DDF_j\left(\vartheta\right) = \tilde{S}\sum_{\varepsilon=0}^{1}\sum_{i=1}^{\Omega} \Lambda_{ij}\left(\vartheta, \varepsilon\right) match\left(\vartheta, B_{ij}\right) \qquad (A.2)$$

that simplifies further as all rotational matrices $R(\theta_i)$ are equal, thus setting $\vartheta = 0$ gives:

132

$$DDF_j\left(\vartheta\right) = \tilde{S} \sum_{\varepsilon=0}^{1} \sum_{i=1}^{\Omega} G_{ij}\Psi_{ij}\left(\varepsilon\right) match\left(\vartheta, B_{ij}\right) \qquad (A.3)$$

where the mean and variance parameters for G are equal for all voters, thus removed from the representation. Let M represent the scale of the ROI where there are $\Omega = M \times M$ discrete nodes and let τ (the distance between nodes) from equation 3.5 equal one. Let M be odd such that there are equal numbers of neighboring nodes along a given orientation. For $\varepsilon = 0$, the number of viable nodes that $match(...)$ the ϑ angular bin with respect to B_{ij} is equal to $M\left(\lfloor\frac{M}{2}\rfloor + 1\right)$ whereas the viable nodes from Ψ_{ij} are M. The $\lfloor...\rfloor$ function represents rounding down, also known as the *floor* function. The overlap between these two binary masks reveals only M common nodes. For $\varepsilon = 1$, B_{ij} has $M\left(\lfloor\frac{M}{2}\rfloor\right)$ viable nodes, whereas Ψ_{ij} has the entire $M \times M$ set as viable. The overlap between these two masks reveals $M\left(\lfloor\frac{M}{2}\rfloor\right)$ viable nodes. Therefore, the viable nodes for both values of ε are depicted in the subset:

$$\Omega' = M\left(\left\lfloor\frac{M}{2}\right\rfloor + 1\right) \qquad (A.4)$$

where $\Omega' \subset \Omega$. Equation A.3 can now be rewritten as:

$$DDF_j\left(\vartheta\right) = \tilde{S} \sum_{i=1}^{\Omega'} G_{ij} \qquad (A.5)$$

Since G is defined to be normalized such that the total number of elements sum to one and since $\Omega' < \Omega$, the DDF_j maximum possible value is bounded and defined by the equation:

$$DDF_j\left(\vartheta\right) < \tilde{S} \qquad (A.6)$$

A.2   Stage Two

Given that there are four paradigms: VC-DDF ballot, VC-IB, RC-DDF ballot and RC-IB, proving the case with the largest possible angular bin increase in turn covers the proof of the remaining paradigms. The inward-ballot paradigms propagate fewer ballots to the receiver on account of their selective criteria as to which voting nodes are aligned with the angular bin in question. This infers that the largest ballot possible sent to a single angular bin at the receiver is from a DDF-ballot method. The update apparatus, equation 3.17, for

133

all stage two paradigms, re-written here for convenience, has a learning coefficient that ranges from $[0, 1]$, therefore, if the $DDF_j^{D,t-1}$ term can be proved to be bounded, then DDF_j^t is bounded as well.

$$DDF_j^t(\vartheta) = \alpha DDF_j^{t-1}(\vartheta) + (1 - \alpha) DDF_j^{D,t-1}(\vartheta) \tag{A.7}$$

DDF^D is defined as equation A.8 for the receiver-centered, DDF-ballot:

$$DDF_j^D(\vartheta) = \sum_{i=1}^{\Omega} \hat{\Lambda}_{ji} DDF_i(\vartheta) \tag{A.8}$$

Let the maximum possible value, S_{max} be the ballot form from each of the voters i, then equation A.8 reduces to:

$$DDF_j^D(\vartheta) = S_{\max} \sum_{i=1}^{\Omega} \hat{\Lambda}_{ji} \tag{A.9}$$

Finally, $\hat{\Lambda}$ is defined to such that the maximum possible sum of the elements equals zero. For example, if ρ_{min} were defined as follows:

$$\rho_{\min} > \sqrt{2} \left\lfloor \frac{M}{2} + 1 \right\rfloor \tag{A.10}$$

then all of the elements of $\hat{\Lambda}$ would be maximized to $\frac{1}{\Omega}$ as per equation 3.12. This would imply:

$$DDF_j^D(\vartheta) = S_{\max} \sum_{i=1}^{\Omega} \frac{1}{\Omega} \tag{A.11}$$

which reduces to:

$$DDF_j^D(\vartheta) = S_{\max} \tag{A.12}$$

Appendix B

Ground truth to Estimate Pairing

This forms the algorithm to pair ground truth (direction, saliency) to the measurement, or *estimate* (direction, saliency).

Input: ground truth data (direction, saliency) and estimate data (direction, saliency). For this algorithm, the directions are converted from angles to indices between ranging from 1 to N, where N is the total number of angular bins.

Output: error measurement between the inputs

1. Define and initialize function variables:

   - $dev_{max} = \frac{1}{2}$ - the maximum angular deviation (See Section 5.1.2)

   - $error = 0$ - initial error sum

   - N_e, $salEst$, $dirEst$ - number of directional estimates and the arrays denotes their saliencies and directions respectively

   - N_g, $salGT$, $dirGT$ - number of directional ground truths and the arrays that denote their saliencies and directions respectively

2. Perform an initial check for special cases

   - if $N_e = 0$ then return the maximum possible error as:

$$error = \sum_{g=1}^{N_g} salGT\,(g) \cdot dev_{max}$$

- else if $N_g = 0$ then return the maximum possible error as:

$$error = \sum_{e=1}^{N_e} salEst\,(e) \cdot dev_{\text{max}}$$

3. Pair each estimate with the closest ground truth. The term closest refers to the least angular difference only. This step will result in each ground truth being paired with possibly zero, one or multiple estimates.

4. For each ground truth that has multiple estimate pairs, identify a single estimate as the closest.

   - If one estimate in particular has the least angular difference, use this one as the ground truth's pair and unpair the remaining estimates.

   - If two or more estimates share the minimum angular difference with the ground truth, chose from those estimates that which has the greatest saliency. Unpair the remaining estimates.

   - In the case where there are two estimates that share both the least angular deviation and saliency, [1] choose one of them and unpair the other.

5. At this point, there are pairs of a single ground truth and estimate as well as potentially unpaired ground truths and unpaired estimates. This is then fed into the error equation as per Equation 5.1, which is reproduced here for convenience.

$$SAE = \sum_{e=1}^{N_e} \left\{ [\,|s\,(e) - s\,(pair\,(e))| + \varepsilon] \left[\frac{dev\,(e,\,pair\,(e))}{N} + \varepsilon \right] - \varepsilon^2 \right\} + \frac{1}{2} \sum_{g=1}^{N_{ug}} |s\,(g)|$$

$$pair\,(e) = \begin{cases} G & \text{if } e \text{ is part of a } pair \text{ with ground truth } G \\ 0 & \text{otherwise} \end{cases}$$

where $s(...)$ returns the saliency of an individual estimate or ground truth, $dev(...)$ calculates the angular difference between a pairing of indices that range from 1 to N. N_{ug} corresponds to the number of *unpaired ground truths* and $varepsilon = 0.1$ such that neither the angular nor saliency difference negates the influence of one another. See Section 5.1.2 for further details on the parameters.

---

[1] There can only be a maximum of two such estimates as there are only two possible positions that have equal deviation from a given angle.

www.ingramcontent.com/pod-product-compliance
Lightning Source LLC
Chambersburg PA
CBHW070730220326

41598CB00024BA/3372